Franklin Bowditch Dexter

Sketch of the History of Yale University by Franklink Bowditch Dexter

Franklin Bowditch Dexter

Sketch of the History of Yale University by Franklink Bowditch Dexter

ISBN/EAN: 9783743350212

Manufactured in Europe, USA, Canada, Australia, Japa

Cover: Foto ©ninafisch / pixelio.de

Manufactured and distributed by brebook publishing software (www.brebook.com)

Franklin Bowditch Dexter

Sketch of the History of Yale University by Franklink Bowditch Dexter

SKETCH OF THE HISTORY

OF

YALE UNIVERSITY

BY

FRANKLIN BOWDITCH DEXTER, M.A.

NEW YORK
HENRY HOLT AND COMPANY
1887

PREFATORY NOTE

THE following Sketch has been compiled to meet the frequent demand, on the part of visitors to New Haven and members of the University, for some brief statement of the earlier history of the institution, which will supplement the accounts of its present condition contained in current annual publications. The aim has been to present the most important facts, accurately and concisely. Sources of further information are indicated in the Appendix.

Yale University, June, 1887.

CONTENTS

Prefatory Note	5
The Founding and the Founders, 1701	7–12
The Collegiate School at Saybrook, 1702–16	13–15
The Settlement at New Haven, 1716–18	16–20
Rector Cutler's Administration, 1719–22	21–23
Rector Williams's Administration, 1725–39	24–26
President Clap's Administration, 1739–66	27–37
Dr. Daggett's Administration, 1766–77	38–40
President Stiles's Administration, 1777–95	41–46
President Dwight's Administration, 1795–1817	47–54
President Day's Administration, 1817–46	55–64
President Woolsey's Administration, 1846–71	65–80
President Porter's Administration, 1871–86	81–93
The University in 1886–87	94–96
Appendix: Statistics	97–101
Bibliography	102–04
Index,	105–08

SKETCH OF THE HISTORY

OF

YALE UNIVERSITY

The Founding and the Founders, 1701

IN 1700 New England contained nearly 100,000 white inhabitants. The needs of this scattered community in the way of higher education were supplied by HARVARD COLLEGE, at Cambridge, founded in 1636 by graduates of English Universities. No other seat of learning graced the British Colonies in America, except the infant College of William and Mary, chartered in 1693.

Massachusetts Bay was naturally the chief patron of Harvard; yet, in proportion to her means and numbers, the sister Colony of Connecticut bore her full share in support of the enterprise. But the two commonwealths diverged to some extent in their theological and political development; and though these diverging tendencies were not glaringly apparent, and need not be emphasized further, they are sufficient, together with the natural considerations of distance and independent life, to explain the movement in the third generation for a separate College in Connecticut.

The first distinct traces of this movement appear in the early summer of the year 1701, in the neighborhood of NEW HAVEN, which had had a dream —dating back to its very foundation—of a College of its own. The chief promoter of the new enterprise was the Rev. JAMES PIERPONT, pastor of the New Haven Church, a Harvard graduate of 1681; while his most trusted coadjutor was the Rev. ABRAHAM PIERSON (Harvard 1668), of Killingworth, now Clinton. There is evidence of careful consultation together in this same summer on the part of these clergymen and sundry of their ministerial neighbors, especially those in the coast towns of the Colony; and also of advice sought from leading laymen elsewhere in Connecticut, and of both ministers and laymen in Boston and Cambridge.

Tradition describes a meeting of a few of these Connecticut pastors at BRANFORD, the next town east of New Haven, about the last of September, 1701, and implies that, to constitute a company of founders, those then met gave (or more probably, for themselves and in the name of their most active associates, agreed to give) a collection of books, as the foundation for a College in the Colony. It is otherwise known that after the date which must be assigned to this meeting, the details as to a

Board of Trustees—of what class of persons, and of how many, it should consist—had not been worked out; so that the transaction at Branford can have gone no further than the adoption of a general policy, to be developed later.

Meantime Pierpont and others had sent on to two Boston friends (Secretary Isaac Addington and Judge Samuel Sewall) a paper of suggestions for a draft of a CHARTER to be procured from the Legislature, which was to meet in New Haven on October 9; and a charter framed after Addington's and Sewall's draft was granted (probably on October 16) in the following terms:—

AN ACT FOR LIBERTY TO ERECT A COLLEGIATE SCHOOL

WHEREAS several well disposed, and Publick spirited Persons of their sincere Regard to & Zeal for upholding & Propagating of the Christian Protestant Religion by a succession of Learned & Orthodox men have expressed by Petition their earnest desires that full Liberty and Priveledge be granted unto certain Undertakers for the founding, suitably endowing & ordering a Collegiate School within his Maj^{ties} Colony of Connecticot wherin Youth may be instructed in the Arts & Sciences who thorough the blessing of Almighty God may be fitted for Publick employment both in Church & Civil State. To the intent therefore that all due incouragement be Given to such Pious Resolutions and that so necessary & Religious an undertakeing may be sett forward, supported & well managed:—

BE IT ENACTED by the Govern^r & Company of the s^d Colony of Connecticot, in General Court now Assembled, And it is enacted & ordained by the Authority of the same that there be & hereby is full Liberty, Right and Priveledge Granted unto the Reverend M^r· James Noyes of Stonnington, M^r· Israel Chauncey of Stratford, M^r· Thomas Buckingham of Saybrook, M^r· Abraham Pierson of Kennelworth, M^r· Samuel Mather of Windsor, M^r·

Samuel Andrew of Millford, Mr. Timothy Woodbridge of Hartford, Mr. James Pierpont of New Haven, Mr. Noadiah Russel of Middletown, Mr. Joseph Webb of Fairfield, being Revrd Ministers of the Gospel & inhabitants within ye s^d Colony, proposed to stand as Trustees, Partners or Undertakers for the s^d School, to them and their successors, To ERECT, form, direct, order, establish, improve and att all times in all suitable wayes for the future to encourage the s^d School in such convenient place or Places, & in such form & manner & under such order & Rules as to them shall seem meet & most conducive to the afores^d end thereof, so as such Rules or Orders be not Repugnant to the Laws of the Civil Governm^t, as also to imploy the moneys or any other estate which shall be Granted by this Court or otherwise Contributed to that use according to their discretion for the benefit of the s^d Collegiate School from time to time & att all times henceforward.

And be it further ENACTED by the Authority afores^d that the before named Trustees, Partners or Undertakers together with such others as they shall associate to themselves (not exceeding the number of Eleven, or att any time being less than Seven, Provided also that Persons nominated or associated from time to time to fill up s^d number be ministers of the gospel inhabiting within this Colony & above the Age of forty years) or the major Part of them, the s^d Mr. James Noyes, [etc.] undertakers, & of such Persons so chosen & associated as aboves^d att any time hereafter, HAVE and shall have henceforward the oversight, full & compleat Right, Liberty, power & Priveledge to furnish, direct, manage, order, improve & encourage from time to time & in all times hereafter the s^d Collegiate School so Erected & formed by them in such ways, orders & manner & by such Persons, Rector or Master and officers appointed by them, as shall according to their best discretion be most conducible to attaine the afores^d mentioned end thereof.

And Moreover it is Enacted & ordered by the Governor, Council & Representatives of ye Colony afores^d met in General Assembly—

That the s^d Mr. James Noyes, [etc.] Undertakers, Trustees or Partners, & ye s^d Persons taken from time to time into Partnership, or associated as afores^d with themselves, shall HAVE & receive & it is hereby GIVEN & GRANTED unto them, the full &

just sum of one hundred & twenty pounds in Country Pay to be paid Annually & att all times hereafter until this Court order otherwise, to them & to such Person or Persons only as they shall appoint & impower to Receiv the same, to be faithfully disposed of by ye s^d Trustees, Partners or Undertakers for the end afores^d according to their discretion, which s^d sum shall be raised & Paid in such ways & manners & att such a value as ye Country Rates of s^d Colony are & have been usually raised & Paid.

It is also further Enacted by the Authority afores^d that the s^d Undertakers & Partners & their successors be & hereby are further impowered to have, accept, acquire, purchase or otherwise lawfully enter upon Any Lands, Tenements & Hereditam^ts to the use of the s^d School, not exceeding the value of five hundred Pounds p^r Anñ, & any Goods, Chattels, Sum or Sums of money whatsoever as have heretofore already been Granted, bestowed, bequeathed or given, or as from time to time shall be freely given, bequeathed, devised or settled by any Person or Persons whatsoever upon & to & for the use of ye s^d School towards the founding, erecting or endowing the same, & to sue for, Recover & receiv all such Gifts, Legacies, bequests, annuities, Rents, issues & profits arising therefrom & to imploy the same accordingly, & out of ye estate, Revenues, Rents, profits, incoms accrueing & belonging to s^d School to support & pay as the s^d Undertakers shall agree & see cause, the s^d Rector or Master, Tutors, Ushers or other officers their Respective annual Salaries or Allowances. As also for the encouragem^t of the Students to grant degrees or Licences as they or those deputed by them shall see cause to order & appoint.

It may be noticed that the charter minimizes the importance of the undertaking; by adopting the designation (recommended by the Boston gentlemen) of a "*Collegiate School*," and by introducing in an almost incidental manner the power of granting degrees; this was doubtless due to the delicate relations of the Colony government to the mother country, and to anxiety to avoid emphasizing any action which might be construed as an invasion of the rights of the crown. That the framers of the instrument comprehended the true scope of their institution is inferrible from the absence of all restrictions on the course of study, not even the religious instruction (which they certainly viewed as essential) being prescribed.

It is also noteworthy that the charter seems to avoid claiming to *found* the School,—as if conceding that the founding was already accomplished by the Undertakers, and in this light also the Act of the Assembly was of slight importance.

The Collegiate School at Saybrook, 1702-16.

ORGANIZATION under the charter took place in November, 1701, when seven trustees met in Saybrook, at the mouth of the Connecticut, and voted to fix the School there, under the Rev. Mr. PIERSON as RECTOR. At the same time a course of theological instruction was sketched out, for the Rector's guidance, while in all respects not specially provided for, in the curriculum and the general administration of the School, the rules of Harvard College were to be followed. In March, 1702, the first student, JACOB HEMINWAY, of New Haven, offered himself, and on September 16 the first Commencement was held, at the house of the Rev. Thomas Buckingham, on Saybrook Point, in the present town of Old Saybrook. At this Commencement the degree of Master of Arts was conferred on four young Harvard Bachelors, and also on NATHANIEL CHAUNCEY, of Stratford, who had been privately educated (presumably by his uncle, one of the Trustees), and whose name thus leads the roll of academical graduates of Yale University.

In this same month of September, more students entered, and a tutor was appointed to assist in instruction. The enterprise depended mainly on the tuition fees from the few students, and the annual grant of £120 in "country pay" (equal to £80 in money) from the Colony Legislature, as promised in the charter; but these revenues would hardly justify the Rector in resigning his parochial charge, so that he was authorized to continue temporarily in Killingworth,—nine miles from Saybrook, where the School was nominally located; and this arrangement continued till his death. Meantime, a small house and lot of land on Saybrook Point were offered (in 1702) by Mr. Nathaniel Lynde for the School's use; and the annual Commencements were always attended in the same locality.

RECTOR PIERSON died, after a brief illness, March 5, 1707, at the age of 61, leaving a reputation for good scholarship and for practical wisdom as an administrator. A manuscript text-book on Natural Philosophy which he drew up was used by the students for a quarter of a century. An oak arm-chair which is believed to have belonged to him is now in the Library of the University.

After Mr. Pierson's death the Rev. SAMUEL ANDREW, of Milford, one of the original Trustees, was put in nominal charge as Rector, but without the expectation that he should remove to Saybrook, where the instruction and discipline of the classes were entrusted to two young tutors. Under this unsatisfactory arrangement the institution languished visibly for six or seven years; but about 1713 efforts were begun for gifts to the School, especially by JEREMIAH DUMMER, the agent for Connecticut at London. As a direct result, nearly 1,000 volumes of great value were sent from England to the Library in 1714-15, many of which can still be identified; among them were gifts from Sir Isaac Newton, Richard Steele, Richard Bentley, Edmund Halley, William Whiston, Edmund Calamy, Matthew Henry, White Kennet, Sir Edmund Andros, Sir Richard Blackmore, and ELIHU YALE. This effort was most important of all in turning Governor Yale's attention to this claimant on his bounty.

These gifts gave point to the petitions addressed by the Trustees to the Colony Assembly for means to build a house to shelter the School and its possessions; and in 1715 a grant of £500 for this object was made, from money to be realized the next year by the payment from Massachusetts for her encroachments on the boundaries of Connecticut.

The Settlement at New Haven, 1716-18

WITH the prospect of a permanent building, the dormant opposition to the present location, both among Trustees and patrons, became manifest. Originally chosen as a convenient center for the coast-towns which had fathered the enterprise, as well as for the river-towns, Saybrook had now to encounter the rivalries of two more populous and in every way more prominent places, Hartford and New Haven. The other Trustees were inclined to abide by Saybrook; but two of the Board who were residents of Hartford so used their influence (not altogether fairly) in favor of their own locality, as to turn a majority of their colleagues to NEW HAVEN, where in the meantime a popular subscription for the College had reached a higher figure than either Saybrook or Hartford could show. The decisive vote was passed in October, 1716, and committees were raised to proceed with the erection of a Rector's house and a College at New Haven in the ensuing spring. Of the two tutors elected along with this vote, one established himself at once in New Haven, in charge of about a dozen pupils; the other, influenced by the Hartford Trustees, opened a rival school, with as many or more pupils, in WETHERSFIELD (the next town south of Hartford), where he had the valuable help of Mr. Elisha Williams, a recent

Harvard graduate (1711), of high repute as an instructor; three or four pupils remained at Saybrook, under the care of the village pastor, a former tutor.

COMMENCEMENT was celebrated at NEW HAVEN for the first time on September 11, 1717; and two weeks later the Trustees bought on easy terms the lot of land on which they had fixed as the site for their new building, namely, 1¼ acres at the southeast corner of what is now the COLLEGE SQUARE. On October 8 the building was raised, and one year from that day it was first occupied. Though of wood, it was architecturally an ambitious structure, the plan having been drawn by Governor Saltonstall; it was about 170 feet long, 22 feet deep, and three stories high, with an attic. Besides a large dining hall (used also as a chapel) and a library, there were twenty-two sets of rooms for students, each of which might accommodate three persons. It is not probable that as many as thirty persons had ever yet been in attendance at the School at any one time; so that this enlarged provision implied the expectation of great future expansion.

Not until the building was actually begun did the Hartford Trustees abandon the hope of defeating the New Haven project by the interference of the Legislature, and not until June, 1719, was the school at Wethersfield finally adjourned to New Haven. The chief agents in frustrating these designs were Governor SALTONSTALL and the Rev. JOHN DAVENPORT, of Stamford, who was the most influential of the Trustees after Pierpont's death in 1714. Another potent friend was the Rev. COTTON MATHER, of Boston, whose father, as well as himself, had been an adviser and helper from the beginning. In January, 1718, Cotton Mather wrote to Elihu Yale, of London, in these memorable words:

"The Colony of Connecticut, having for some years had a College at Saybrook without a collegious way of living for it, have lately begun to erect a large edifice for it in the town of New Haven. The charge of that expensive building is not yet all paid, nor are there yet any funds of revenues for salaries to the Professors and instructors to the society. Sir, though you have your felicities in your family, which I pray God to continue and multiply, yet certainly, if what is forming at New Haven might wear the name of YALE COLLEGE, it would be better than a name of sons and daughters."

The result of this application, seconded by DUMMER'S visits, was seen in the arrival at Boston, late in August, of a cargo of gifts from Governor YALE; besides a large box of books and a portrait of the King (still preserved), there were East India goods inventoried at £200, from which was realized in the Boston market £562. 12s. sterling. These gifts were sent for the benefit of the Collegiate School *at New Haven;* and neither quibbling by individuals nor legislation by the Colony could divert the proceeds from their plain use. No wonder then that the Commencement of 1718 was a jubilant one, nor that the gratitude of the Trustees led them to apply the name of YALE COLLEGE to the institution in its new domicil.

The donor thus commemorated was himself of New Haven stock. His father, David Yale, had taken part as a youth in the founding of the town (as a member of the family of his step-father, Governor Theophilus Eaton), but had soon migrated to Boston, where ELIHU YALE is supposed to have been born in 1648. Thence the family returned to England, and about 1670 the son went to India to seek his fortune. He found employment under the East India Company, rose rapidly to the place of Governor or President of the settlement at Madras, and in 1699 came back to England, enormously rich, but without a son to inherit his wealth. The University owns a copy of his portrait, at full-length, presented by his last living descendant, a great-grandson, in 1789.

By these events of 1718 the College was unalterably fixed at New Haven, yet one struggle remained: Saybrook was unconvinced. The Colonial Assembly endeavored indeed to soothe the feelings of the disappointed towns by voting (October, 1718) a gratuity of £50 to the public school in Saybrook, and £500 for building a State House in Hartford; at the same time they requested the Governor and his Council to take all necessary steps for the safe removal to New Haven of the College property still in Saybrook. The chief part of this property was the library, of perhaps 1300 volumes, and the records of the Trustees; but the angry gentleman in whose hands these had been left persisted in ignoring any claim made in behalf of "Yale College" to the assets of the Collegiate School, and his neighbors supported him in this attitude. By the sheriff's aid the requisition was carried into effect, but only after a disgraceful series of outrages, at least one-fifth of the library being lost in the process, as well as all the records of the Trustees for the Saybrook period of their history.

Rector Cutler's Administration, 1719–22

THE most obvious remaining weakness of the College was the immaturity of its instructors; accordingly, the next concern of the Trustees was to secure a resident Rector worthy of confidence. The person selected, not without misgivings, was the Rev. TIMOTHY CUTLER (Harvard 1701), a son-in-law of Rector Andrew, about 35 years of age, who had been for nine years settled over the Congregational Church in Stratford, Connecticut. He had made a favorable impression for ability, and readily accepted the offer of employment as Rector, which was given him in March, 1719. The appointment did not require an election into the number of the Trustees, for which indeed Mr. Cutler's age disqualified him, not to speak of other grounds of hesitation.

Now that the office of Rector was filled, the project of building a house for his occupation was revived, and was carried into effect by the completion in the summer of 1722 of a substantial mansion, near the site of the present College Street Church, which was used by the successive Presidents to the close of the century. One fifth of the expense of this house and the adjoining land was met by a second gift sent by Governor Yale shortly before his death in 1721; a somewhat larger portion came from private subscriptions and a collection taken in the churches of the Colony; the balance was a gift by the Assembly from the proceeds of the tax on rum.

But just as the new house was finished, the Rector's usefulness came to a sudden end. After some rumors of strange doctrinal teachings, it was made known at the Commencement, in September, 1722, that the Rector and the Tutor then in office, with five neighboring ministers, were considering the question of declaring for Episcopacy. At that date the Church of England had few avowed members in Connecticut, and not a single gathered congregation. An itinerant Episcopal missionary had lately been in conference with the Rector and his friends, but it is asserted that even before leaving Stratford Cutler had contemplated such a change, so that the leisure and opportunities for reading afforded at the College had only aided an existing inclination. However this may have been, it is certain that he did not announce his purpose at New Haven, until in receipt of overtures from a new Episcopal church in Boston to become their minister,—an arrangement which was immediately consummated. There were still on the stage the children of those who had participated in the planting of New England by Puritans fleeing from persecution in the Established Church; and words can hardly overstate the dismay caused by this perversion of the accredited guides of instruction in the College. The Rector was immediately " excused from all further service;" the Tutor's resignation was accepted; and provision was made for subscription on the part of all officers of instruction henceforth to a test of theological soundness,—a provision which was retained in one form or another until 1823. On this new basis two tutors were chosen and inducted into office, and the Trustees bent their energies to the selection of a new Rector. They found themselves hampered by the fact that one of their number (Samuel Mather) had long been mentally and bodily disabled, but was not removable under their charter; accordingly they asked the Assembly's advice on this and some other doubtful points in their constitution. The result was the passage of an "ADDITIONAL ACT," in October, 1723, authorizing the supply of vacancies caused by resignation or incapacity, and also constituting the Rector *ex-officio* a Trustee, and lowering the limit of age required to thirty years. The first provision was put in force at once; and the next Rector succeeded to the first vacancy occurring in the Board after his entrance on office.

Rector Williams's Administration, 1725-39

THE Rector chosen in September, 1725, after wide search, was the same Rev. ELISHA WILLIAMS who had drawn off to Wethersfield, in the break-up at Saybrook, so large a portion of the Collegiate School. After having served in the Assembly with credit, he had lately been settled as pastor of a new parish (Newington) in Wethersfield, and he was commended for the Rectorship by his known success in teaching, his acquaintance and wide popularity among civilians as well as among the clergy, and the prominence of his family in the whole Connecticut valley.

Rector Williams gave himself for fourteen years, from the age of 31, to the work of teaching and government in the College, with fidelity and evident success. It may be doubted whether the position aroused the full use of his powers; certainly the versatility and sagacity which have been remarked as his chief characteristics, attach more truly to the later portion of his life, during which (until his death in his 61st year) he figured with distinction and authority at a critical time in Connecticut politics, serving with credit both in judicial and in military stations, as well as in embassies to the mother country and in the most important intercolonial conferences of that generation.

Under his wise administration of the College there was a steady enlargement of resources, chiefly by a series of extra grants from the government, which justified an increase in the teaching force by the addition of a second tutor in 1728. One interesting detail of internal policy which dates from this time is the appointment by the Trustees (in 1737) of a Standing Committee of their own number, out of which has grown the PRUDENTIAL COMMITTEE, the working body of the Corporation for the last ninety years.

The most notable incident of Rector Williams's time was the succession of valuable gifts received in 1731-33 from the liberal-minded GEORGE BERKELEY, Dean of Derry and afterwards Bishop of Cloyne, who came to Rhode Island in 1729 in the hope of founding a College in Bermuda; on returning to England after the failure of this scheme, he conveyed to Yale College, as a foundation for graduate scholarships and undergraduate prizes, his estate of "Whitehall," near Newport, and also sent a choice collection of books—about nine hundred volumes—for the Library. Such interest in a College controlled by nonconformists may be wondered at in a Churchman (though Governor Yale was a Churchman also), but is explained by the character of the man and the circumstances, and particularly by the friendship which had sprung up between Berkeley and the Rev. SAMUEL JOHNSON, of Stratford, a Yale graduate (1714) and quondam tutor, who had gone over to Episcopacy with Rector Cutler, but was still, while the senior Episcopal missionary in the Colony, sincerely interested in the progress of his *alma mater.* The Berkeley Scholarships and Prizes are still annually offered, though the income of the former ($55 a year) is disappointingly small,—the Dean's farm having been leased for a term of 999 years in 1763, with an unfortunate lack of foresight of the change in value of real estate in the neighborhood of Newport.

The University owns an interesting painting of Berkeley and his family, by John Smibert, himself one of the group and a pioneer in the history of American art.

Many of the books which Berkeley gave are still in the Library, though a considerable part of the invoice consisted of duplicate copies of standard editions of the classics, which were designed for use as text-books and consequently have long since disappeared.

President Clap's Administration, 1739-66

RECTOR WILLIAMS resigned his office, on account of impaired health, in October, 1739, and the Trustees at once elected to the vacant place the Rev. THOMAS CLAP, who was inducted into office in April, 1740. The new Rector was a native of Scituate, in Massachusetts, and a graduate of Harvard (1722). He had been for thirteen years pastor of the church in Windham, Connecticut, and was now in the 37th year of his age. His administration extended until September, 1766, and was thus one of the longest which the College has known; nor has any administration been more eventful. He had already made a mark among the younger ministry of the Colony by his vigorous course in matters of church-government; and he was acceptable to the Trustees and the public from the expectation that he would bring abundant energy and practical sense to the service of 'the College, as well as exact scholarship. Nor were these expectations disappointed. His activity wrought as a new impulse at every point of the College interests. He made himself felt as an administrator outside, by securing an extension of the chartered powers of the College, by successfully resisting and for all time to come overthrowing an attempt at visitatorial interference, and by withdrawing the College congregation—in the face of violent opposition—

from the New Haven Church to a separate position inside the College walls; in like manner, within his proper domain, his administrative qualities shone, in the systematization and more thorough application of the laws for the students, in the broadening of the course of study, in the development of the tutorial and the introduction of the professorial system, in the increase of funds, and in the multiplication of buildings.

The earlier years of his term of office were years of religious agitation, and Rector Clap proved an ardent supporter of the government policy of repression of all " Separatist " congregations and " New-Light " revival movements.

The evidences of his vigor and of his orthodoxy were at first generally acceptable, and the Rector was thus able to secure an augmentation of the Colony grant in 1743, which justified the addition of a third tutor to the staff of instruction.

A more important fruit of the confidence had in him was the passage in 1745 without change of a new CHARTER which he had drafted, and which still does credit to his sagacity. The Charter is as follows :—

WHEREAS upon the Petition of several well disposed and public-spirited Persons expressing their desire that full Liberty and Privilege might be granted unto certain Undertakers for the founding, suitably endowing and ordering a *Collegiate School*, within this Colony, wherein Youth might be instructed in the Arts and Sciences, the Governor and Company of the said Colony in General Court assembled at *New Haven*, on the Ninth Day of October, in the Year of our Lord One Thousand Seven Hundred and One, Granted unto the Rev'd Messrs. *James Noyes*.

[etc.], who were proposed to stand as Trustees, Partners or Undertakers for the Society, and to their Successors, full Liberty, Right and Privilege to erect, form, direct, order, establish, improve, and at all Times in all suitable Ways to encourage the said School in some convenient Place in this Colony, and granted sundry Powers and Privileges for the attaining the End aforesaid:

And Whereas the said Trustees, Partners or Undertakers in pursuance of the aforesaid Grant, Liberty and License, founded a *Collegiate School* at *New Haven* known by the Name of YALE COLLEGE, which has received the favorable Benefactions of many liberal and piously disposed Persons, and under the Blessing of Almighty God has trained up many worthy Persons for the Service of God in the State as well as in the Church;

And Whereas the General Court of this Colony assembled at *New Haven*, the Tenth Day of October, in the Year of our Lord One Thousand Seven Hundred and Twenty Three, did explain and enlarge the aforesaid Powers and Privileges granted to the aforesaid Partners, Trustees or Undertakers and their Successors, for the Purpose aforesaid; as by the respective Acts, reference thereto being had, more fully and at large may appear;

And Whereas the Rev'd Messrs. *Thomas Clap, Samuel Whitman, Jared Eliot, Ebenezer Williams, Jonathan Marsh, Samuel Cooke, Samuel Whittelsey, Joseph Noyes, Anthony Stoddard, Benjamin Lord,* and *Daniel Wadsworth*, the present Trustees, Partners and Undertakers of the said School, and Successors of those beforementioned, have petitioned, that the said School, with all the Rights, Powers, Privileges and Interests thereof, may be confirmed, and that such other additional Powers and Privileges may be granted as shall be necessary for the Ordering and Managing the said School in the most advantageous and beneficial Manner for the promoting all good Literature in the present and succeeding Generations:

Therefore,

THE GOVERNOR and COMPANY of his Majesty's said English Colony of *Connecticut* in General Court assembled, this Ninth Day of *May*, in the Year of our Lord One Thousand Seven Hundred and Forty Five, enact, ordain, and declare, and by these Presents it is enacted, ordained and declared—

1. That the said *Thomas Clap*, [etc.], shall be an *Incorporate Society* or *Body Corporate and Politic*, and shall hereafter be called and known by the name of THE PRESIDENT AND FELLOWS OF YALE COLLEGE IN NEW HAVEN, and that by the same Name they and their Successors shall and may have perpetual Succession, and shall and may be Persons in the Law capable to plead and be impleaded, defend and be defended, and answer and be answered unto ; and also to have, take, possess, acquire, purchase or otherwise receive Lands, Tenements, Hereditaments, Goods, Chattels or other Estates, and the same Lands, Tenements, Hereditaments, Goods, Chattels, or other Estates to grant, demise, lease, use, manage or improve for the Good and Benefit of the said *College*, according to the Tenor of the Donation, and their Discretion.

2. That all Gifts, Grants, Bequests, and Donations of Lands, Tenements or Hereditaments, of Goods and Chattels heretofore made to or for the Use, Benefit and Advantage of the *Collegiate School* aforesaid, whether the same be expressed to be made to the President or Rector, and to the rest of the Incorporate Society of *Yale College*, or to the Trustees or Undertakers of the *Collegiate School* in *New Haven*, or to the Trustees by any other Name, Style or Title whatsoever, whereby it may be clearly known and understood that the true Intent and Design of such Gifts, Grants, Bequests and Donations, was to or for the Use, Benefit and Advantage of the Collegiate School aforesaid, and to be under the Care and Disposal of the Governors thereof, shall be confirmed, and the same hereby are confirmed, and shall be and remain to, and be vested in the President and Fellows of the *College* aforesaid, and their Successors, as to the true and lawful Successors of the original Grantees.

3. That the said PRESIDENT AND FELLOWS and their Successors shall and may hereafter have a common Seal, to serve and use for all Causes, Matters and Affairs of them and their Successors, and the same Seal to alter, break and make new as they shall think fit.

4. That the said THOMAS CLAP shall be, and he is hereby established the present PRESIDENT, and the said *Samuel Whitman*, [etc.], shall be, and they are hereby established the present FELLOWS of the said College, and that they and their Successors shall continue in their respective Places during Life, or until they or either of them shall resign, or be removed, or displaced, as in this Act is hereafter expressed.

5. That there shall be a General Meeting of the *President and Fellows* of said *College*, in the College Library on the second Wednesday of September annually, or at any other Time and Place which they shall see Cause to appoint, to consult, advise and act in and about the Affairs and Business of the said College ; and that on any special Emergency, the President and two of the Fellows, or any four of the Fellows, may appoint a Meeting at the said College, provided they give Notice thereof to the Rest by Letters sent and left with them, or at the Places of their respective Abode, five Days before such Meeting ; and that the President and six Fellows, or in Case of the Death, Absence, or Incapacity of the President, seven Fellows, convened as aforesaid (in which Case the eldest Fellow shall preside), shall be deemed a Meeting of the President and Fellows of said College, and that in all the said Meetings, the Major Vote of the Members present shall be deemed the Act of the Whole, and where an Equivote happens, the President shall have a casting Vote.

6. That the President and Fellows of the said College and their Successors, in any of their Meetings assembled as aforesaid, shall and may from Time to Time, as Occasion shall require, elect and appoint a President or Fellow in the Room and Place of any President or Fellow who shall die, resign, or be removed from his Office, Place or Trust (whom the said Governor and Company hereby declare, for any Misdemeanor, Unfaithfulness, Default or Incapacity, shall be removable by the President and Fellows of the said College ; Six of them, at least, concurring in such Act) ; and shall have power to appoint a Scribe or Register, a Treasurer, Tutors, Professors, Steward and all such other Officers and Servants, usually appointed in Colleges or Universities, as they shall find necessary and think fit to appoint for the promoting good Literature, and the well ordering and managing the Affairs of said College ; and them or any of them, at their Discretion, to remove ; and to prescribe and administer such Forms of Oaths (not being contrary to the Laws of England or of this Colony) as they shall think proper, to be administered to all the Officers and Instructors of the said College, or to such and so many of them as they shall think proper, for the faithful Execution of their respective Places, Offices and Trusts.

7. That the present President and Fellows of said College and their Successors, and all such Tutors, Professors and other Offi-

cers, as shall be appointed for the public Instruction and Government of said College, before they undertake the Execution of their respective Offices and Trusts, or within three Months after, shall publicly in the College-Hall take the Oaths and subscribe the Declaration appointed by an Act of Parliament made in the first Year of KING GEORGE 1st., Entitled, an *Act for the further Security of his Majesty's Person and Government, and the Succession of the Crown in the Heirs of the late Princess* Sophia, *being Protestants, and for extinguishing the Hopes of the Pretended Prince of Wales, and his open and secret Abettors ;* that is to say, the President before the Governor, Deputy-Governor, or any two of the Assistants of this Colony, for the Time being; and the Fellows, Tutors and other Officers before the President, for the Time being, who is hereby impowered to administer the same; an entry of all which shall be made in the Records of said College.

8. That the President and Fellows shall have the Government, Care and Management of the said College and all the Matters and Affairs thereunto belonging, and shall have Power from Time to Time, as Occasion shall require, to make, ordain and establish all such wholesome and reasonable Laws, Rules and Ordinances, not repugnant to the Laws of England, nor the Laws of this Colony, as they shall think fit and proper for the Instruction and Education of the Students, and Ordering, Governing, Ruling and Managing the said College, and all Matters, Affairs, and Things thereunto belonging, and the same to Repeal and alter as they shall think fit; which shall be laid before this Assembly as often as required, and may also be repealed or disallowed by this Assembly when they shall think proper.

9. That the President of said College, with the Consent of the Fellows, shall have Power to give and confer all such Honors, Degrees or Licenses as are usually given in Colleges or Universities, upon such as they shall think worthy thereof.

10. That all the Lands and Ratable Estate belonging to the said College, not exceeding the yearly Value of Five Hundred Pounds Sterling, lying in this Government, and the Persons, Families and Estates of the President and Professors, lying and being in the Town of *New Haven*, and the Persons of the Tutors, Students and such and so many of the Servants of said College as give their constant Attendance on the Business of it, shall be freed and exempted from all Rates, Taxes, Military-

Service, Working at Highways, and other such like Duties and Services.

11. And for the special Encouragement and Support of said College, this Assembly do hereby Grant unto the said President and Fellows and their Successors, for the Use of the said College, in Lieu of all former Grants, One Hundred Pounds Silver Money, at the Rate of Six Shillings and Eight Pence per Ounce, to be paid in Bills of public Credit or other Currency equivalent to the said Hundred Pounds (the Rate or Value thereof to be stated from Time to Time by this Assembly) in two equal Payments, in October and May annually, this payment fo continue during the Pleasure of this Assembly.

IN FULL TESTIMONY AND CONFIRMATION of this Grant and all the Articles and Matters therein contained, the said Governor and Company do hereby order that this Act shall be signed by the Governor and Secretary and sealed with the Public Seal of the Colony, and that the same or a Duplicate or Exemplification thereof shall be a sufficient Warrant to the said President and Fellows to hold, use and exercise all the Powers and Privileges therein mentioned and contained.

The instrument above recited legalized the name "YALE COLLEGE," and in general provided a more explicit and liberal statement of the powers and privileges conferred in 1701 and 1723; the change of titles from Rector and Trustees to PRESIDENT AND FELLOWS was a natural corollary from the College name, but this change involved another of much more consequence, the exaltation of the President to the leadership of the Corporation, while the Rector of former days was only one of a body of equal powers; the grant of the power of removal of a Fellow, while in any case defensible and desirable, was a direct result of Clap's personality and of existing theological differences.

The next great achievement of President Clap's administration was the building of a brick College —now known as SOUTH MIDDLE COLLEGE—in 1750-52, at an expense of £1660 sterling, on land which he purchased to the north of the former College building. The Colony Legislature provided most of the necessary funds, from an authorized lottery, from the proceeds of the sale of a captured French prize, and from some miscellaneous debts due to the government.

Before this building was finished, the President had become obnoxious to many of his former friends by his course in regard to the religious position of the College. It had been the custom hitherto for the students, both undergraduate and graduate (for there were usually a number of graduates in residence, pursuing advanced studies, especially in divinity, during the three years which intervened between the B.A. and M.A. degrees), to attend on Sunday the First Church in New Haven,—morning and evening prayers being the only religious services maintained by the College authorities. The pastor of the First Church, the Rev. Joseph Noyes, had become in the course of years extremely unpopnlar from his dull preaching and the vagueness of his doctrinal statements. Under these circumstances it happened that in 1745 the Hon. Col. PHILIP LIVINGSTON, of the Manor of Livingston, in New York Province, four of whose sons had been educated here, gave to the College a small sum of money (£28. 10s. sterling), and in response to Clap's apprehensions of unorthodox influences on the students the Corporation voted in 1746 to appropriate this sum to a fund for a PROFESSORSHIP OF DIVINITY. The realization of the scheme was not urged for several years, but in 1752 the Board proceeded to an election, which was declined. The President was then directed (November, 1753) to hold regular Sunday services in the College Hall, and the separation from the town congregation was definitely made, though loudly denounced as a schismatical act; at the same time stringent declarations were adopted, expressing, and securing for the future, the adherence of the College government to the Westminster and Saybrook standards. Finally, in 1755, the Rev. NAPHTALI DAGGETT, of Smithtown, Long Island, a graduate of seven years' standing, was installed in the Professorship, and in 1757–58 the College built a house for him and his successors in office, on a lot of land on York street (on part of which the Medical College now stands), given for the purpose by the President, the funds for the building being also obtained through his solicitations. In 1757 a COLLEGE CHURCH of twelve members (eight of them undergraduates) was organized, and in 1761 the great undertaking of erecting a brick CHAPEL and Library (now the Athenaeum) was begun; all the available College funds were absorbed in this enterprise, and large private subscriptions were procured by the indefatigable President, but a deficit nevertheless remained.

Meantime this series of measures had provoked

much criticism, and as early as 1755 a pamphlet war against the new policy was begun. One result was the refusal, in May, 1755, of the Colony Assembly to pass the usual grant to the College; and this withdrawal of the support offered in the Charter crippled the institution severely for the rest of this administration. No less alarming was the proposal of a VISITATION by the Colony authorities, openly made by some members of the Corporation as early as 1758 (in consequence of Clap's arbitrary overriding of a minority of that body), and pushed to the test in 1763 by representative clergymen and laymen in a formal memorial to the Assembly. The memorialists were represented by two of the ablest lawyers of the day, whom the President single-handed met in argument and vanquished triumphantly, notwithstanding his own unpopularity. He made a convincing defence of the independent right of the Corporation, as representatives of the founders, to manage the concerns of the College, without being amenable to visitation by the Assembly; his masterly effort, which proved that he might have gained high rank at the bar, anticipated in its essence the more celebrated Dartmouth College Case, of the next century.

Besides these public contentions, the President was harassed by a growing spirit of disorder among the students (especially from 1760), fomented by enemies of the College and of his administration, and aided by the unfortunate inefficiency of some of the tutors.

Finally, wearied with cares and oppressed by the approach of age and infirmity, he voluntarily resigned his office at the Commencement of 1766; he survived his resignation less than four months, dying in New Haven on the 7th of January, 1767, in his 64th year. His administration as a whole excited great feeling against the College as well as against himself, and left results of permanent alienation; yet it was undeniably fruitful in vital improvements and promotive of the true interests of the institution. One distinct claim of President Clap to grateful remembrance is his preparation of a small volume of Annals of the College History, which was published in 1766, and is for many and most important particulars our only authority. Another special service to literary history was the publication in 1743 of a classified Catalogue of the Library, which then contained about 2600 volumes, and was strong in classics, theology, and science, and fairly good in English literature.

Dr. Daggett's Administration, 1766-77

PRESIDENT CLAP'S retirement left the College in no condition to provoke further controversy; and among the first results were the hesitating, but as it proved temporary, renewal of grants by the Colony Assembly, and some improvement in College order. The Corporation elected to the Presidency one of their own number, the Rev. JAMES LOCKWOOD (Yale 1735), who declined the office, nominally on other grounds, but really it is believed because of the uncertain financial prospects of the College, particularly in view of the state of the country.

The Corporation then took the natural step of committing the duties of the Presidency, *pro tempore*, to the only permanent member of the Faculty, the Professor of Theology, the Rev. NAPHTALI DAGGETT; and this arrangement continued for ten and a half years,—from October, 1766, to March, 1777. The feeling of suspense attaching to a temporary administration, the unsettled condition of public affairs, and some infelicities in Dr. Daggett's mode of conducting discipline, conspired to make this period one of comparatively small progress; it was remarkable, however for a succession of brilliant young men (including Joseph Howe, John Trumbull, Timothy Dwight, and Joseph Buckminster) who filled the tutorial office, and inspired their students with new zeal for learning and new subjects of thought.

President Clap had been especially proficient in Mathematics and Natural Philosophy, and had given particular attention to those studies in the College. One result, therefore, of his removal was to make manifest a deficiency in this department, and the Corporation were prompted in 1770 to establish a second Professorship in the institution, embracing the above-named branches,—with the hope (which was disappointed) that the Legislature would reward this evidence of progress by a liberal grant. The Rev. NEHEMIAH STRONG, a graduate of 1755, formerly a tutor, and more recently pastor of the church in East Granby, Connecticut, was appointed to the Professorship, and filled the position until December, 1781.

One incidental change under this administration, in part a result of the march of public sentiment, but also in its way a witness of the difference in spirit between Presidents Clap and Daggett, was the adoption, late in the year 1767, of an alphabetical arrangement in all class-lists of students, where hitherto the names had been placed in the supposed order of family rank or respectability; the Triennial Catalogue still retains the latter arrangement for the classes down to 1767. Another evidence of the democratic tendencies of the period is seen in the formation in 1768 of a new literary Society among the students, called the BROTHERS IN UNITY, the name indicating a new spirit, in opposition to that which was attributed to the older LINONIAN SOCIETY, which dated from 1753; these two Societies exercised a large influence in the development of student character, down to the time of their gradual decadence, from about 1850, owing to the growth of smaller, class societies.

As early as 1771 the students began to manifest a restless spirit under the unpopular control of Dr. Daggett; this spirit continued, and his refusal in March, 1777, to discharge any longer the office of President was probably a wise solution of existing difficulties. The chief duty for which he had been called to the College was that of a preacher, and in this by general consent he was satisfactory; but neither his natural gifts nor his acquisitions fitted him for the different task of directing the policy of the institution and of controlling and instructing the students, in a time of special difficulty.

President Stiles's Administration, 1777-95

AT Commencement in 1777 the Fellows with the general approval of the public elected to the vacant office of President the Rev. Dr. EZRA STILES, a graduate of 1746, who had long and successfully served as Tutor, being greatly trusted by President Clap, whose devotion to the College he seemed to have inherited. For over twenty years he had been pastor of a church in Newport, Rhode Island, and in that most cosmopolitan of American towns had found unequaled opportunities for slaking his thirst for universal knowledge. Driven from Newport by the war, he was now ministering to a congregation in Portsmouth, New Hampshire, which would gladly have retained him as their pastor; but a sense of duty led him to accept the offer of the Corporation, although not removing to the College until June, 1778.

He found the students much demoralized by irregular residence during the past two years—the early period of the REVOLUTION—in which the College had been practically broken up and the several classes scattered in different localities, owing to the derangement of finances and the want of provisions, which had made it almost impossible to keep up College commons. Dr. Stiles was himself an ardent patriot, and had been among the first to welcome the prospect of independence. He accepted the Presidency with the understanding that efforts should be made to bring about a closer union of the College and the State government, and in this hope he persevered through the trying days of the Revolution and the Confederation. He was early deprived of the aid of the two Professors whom he found in office, in each case in a measure by the intervention of public events. Dr. Daggett, when the British in September, 1779, invaded the town, shouldered a musket for its defense, and his death fourteen months later was in part a result of ill-treatment experienced on being taken prisoner at this time. Professor Strong, on the other hand, was too much of a loyalist to be thoroughly at ease in the patriotic atmosphere of the College, and after long-continued complaints of inadequate support (a necessary result of the disasters of the times) he resigned his place in December, 1781.

The instruction of the Senior class in Mental and Moral Philosophy was a part of the President's duties, and Dr. Stiles, in accepting the office, had expressed a desire for special recognition of additional instruction which he proposed to give, and accordingly had been constituted Professor of Ecclesiastical History, as well as President, both which offices he retained until his death. He by no means, however, confined himself to these duties; and during the long intervals (the most of his administration) in which the other Professorships were actually or practically vacant, the President was competent to fill those also. To the Professorship vacated by Mr. Strong no appointment was made for thirteen years; and during all this time the President usually gave lectures once or twice a week on the more important topics in Mathematics, Natural Philosophy, and Astronomy. The Professorship of Divinity, having some endowment, was more easy to supply, and in June, 1782, the Rev. SAMUEL WALES, a graduate of 1767, for a short time a tutor, and since 1770 the eloquent pastor of a church in the adjoining town of Milford, was inducted as Dr. Daggett's successor; but in 1783, on the threshold of a promising career, a nervous disorder attacked him, from which he was never again entirely free, and which after ten years of partial disability caused his retirement. Thus the duties of this Professorship also—including a regular course in theology for graduates and undergraduates, and the supply of the Chapel pulpit—devolved on President Stiles during much of his term of office.

This multiplicity of labors was further increased by the considerable increase in the number of students, the places of those who were diverted into the ranks of the army being more than filled by those who wished to profit by the exemption from military service secured by law to members of the College community. Thus, at the close of the war, in 1783, there were 270 undergraduates on the rolls, as against 132 in 1777, and 139 in 1787.

A few contributions to the permanent resources of the College cheered these dismal years. In May, 1781, the Rev. Dr. RICHARD SALTER, of Mansfield, Connecticut, a former Fellow of the Corporation, conveyed to the College a tract of land, the avails of which (now amounting to $3,700) were to endow a Professorship of Hebrew and other Oriental languages,—another department of learning in which the versatile President was notably proficient. In January, 1782, by the death of Dr. DANIEL LATHROP (Yale, 1733), of Norwich, Connecticut, the College received a bequest of £500 sterling, to be kept as a permanent fund; and in 1791 a bequest amounting to $1,122, for the benefit of the Library, was made by the Rev. Dr. SAMUEL LOCKWOOD (Yale, 1745), of Andover, Connecticut, who had also given £100 in 1787 to a fund (which reached £300) for the purchase of new philosophical apparatus.

It should be noted that the Library had suffered serious losses in the Revolutionary period under the alarms of invasion and during the dispersion of the students to inland towns.

In the fall of 1782 a new brick building was erected, at an expense of nearly £600 saved from the interest of College funds, in the rear of the other buildings, for use as a common DINING HALL and kitchen, but later known as the Chemical Laboratory. The original College, erected in 1717–18 in front of the present South College, having fallen into decay, through delay of suitable repairs, had been in part pulled down in the winter of 1775–76; but the hall and kitchen at the south end were retained, until superseded by the new hall just mentioned.

It was not till near the close of Dr. Stiles's administration, that his hope of a closer UNION WITH THE STATE was realized. In the earlier years, in spite of his urgent desire for such a consummation, the College was occasionally the subject of malicious comments in the public press, of pamphlet attacks, and of memorials to the legislature, of the same general type as those in President Clap's time, though without a similar infusion of personal spite.

Finally, in 1792, when substantial aid seemed absolutely essential to enable the institution to go on, on the favorable report of a committee which had conferred with the Corporation and had been given every means for a full knowledge of College affairs and their management, the Legislature adopted a plan suggested by the Hon. JAMES HILLHOUSE, the Treasurer of the College, by which in return for a grant of money from the State Treasury (eventually amounting to $40,629) the Governor, the Lieutenant-Governor, and the six senior members of the Upper House for the time being, became *ex-officio* members of the Corporation. This met the outside demand for State oversight of the College, and was at the same time acceptable to the President and the clerical Fellows; the new arrangement took effect by the ratification of the old Corporation in June, 1792, and its wisdom was sufficiently justified by the advantage experienced.

As the first result, the want of more accommodations for students was met by the erection in 1793-94 of a new College dormitory,—the present

SOUTH COLLEGE; and in October, 1794, the long dormant Professorship of Mathematics and Natural Philosophy was filled by the appointment of JOSIAH MEIGS, Esq., a graduate of 1778, who had just returned from a residence in Bermuda as a practitioner of the law, and who while tutor in the College some years before had shown special aptitude for these studies.

In the midst of this returning prosperity, Dr. Stiles's career was ended by an attack of fever, on May 12, 1795, in the 68th year of his age. He had devoted his matured powers unremittingly for seventeen years in a difficult time to the service of the College, and had seen it advance steadily in solid usefulness and in popular reputation.

Though genuinely simple in his private character, he was punctilious about the details of official dignity, and fostered in the true antiquarian spirit all the traditional orders and ceremonies of the place. His religious character was peculiarly humble and charitable; but he was distinctly less rigidly orthodox than President Clap, and had delayed his acceptance of the Presidency until the elaborate tests exacted by the Corporation (who were much of Clap's way of thinking) from College officers, should be modified to a simple assent to the Saybrook Platform.

President Dwight's Administration, 1795–1817

THOUGH the death of Dr. Stiles was sudden, the Fellows were prompt in agreeing on a successor,—one to whom, indeed, the friends of the College instinctively turned at this juncture. This was the Rev. TIMOTHY DWIGHT, D.D., now in his 44th year, who had served with unprecedented success in the tutorship for the last half of Dr. Daggett's Presidency, and at the ensuing election but for his youth would have been a leading candidate for the vacant office. He had now been for twelve years pastor of the church at Greenfield Hill, Connecticut, and for almost the whole time had conducted a flourishing academy, in which the course of study was not merely preparatory to but parallel with the College course of that day.

Dr. Dwight accepted the election, and entered on his office at Commencement, 1795. His predecessor was a typical scholar and divine of the ancient Puritan stamp, an autocrat in his little kingdom, who clung to all the forms and usages of earlier generations; and the change to Dr. Dwight was like the passage from a type of the eighteenth century to an earnest of the nineteenth. In illustration of this change may be adduced the spirit of the revision of the Laws for the students, in 1795, which recognized for the first time as a vital part of the College government the action of the FACULTY, *i.e.*, of the Professors and Tutors sitting in consultation with the President. At a later date (1804) the ancient system of fagging was abolished, and a little later the system of pecuniary fines as a mode of punishment was also given up. A man of grandly impressive personality, most stimulating as an instructor, and movingly eloquent as a preacher, Dr. Dwight's direct influence on the students was much more powerful than that exerted by any of his predecessors. It was not the intention, when he was chosen President, to commit to him also the College pastorate; in fact, as an ardent exponent of the theology of his grandfather, Jonathan Edwards, he was not quite in harmony with the prevailing views among the Fellows who had elected him; but delays occurred in filling the Professorship of Divinity, and meantime the President had temporary charge of the duty, and the vast influence for good which thus opened before him began to be exercised and appreciated. Popular infidelity was met and vanquished; the feeble life of the College church was revived and built up; and the result was that after having officiated by temporary arrangement until 1805, he was then formally invited to the chair of Divinity, which he held with the Presidency till his death. Besides these duties he gave the full attention expected from the President to the usual studies of the senior year in philosophy, and also did much to create a new department of instruction, that of Rhetoric and English Literature, for which he had shown special adaptation as early as his tutorship.

While he thus most powerfully impressed himself on the students before him, he was quite as successful in perpetuating his influence by a rare sagacity of insight into the capacities and promise of those whom he selected for permanent positions in the Faculty. This was most strikingly illustrated by the careers of three young men whom he called around him early in his term of office:—Jeremiah Day, appointed Professor of Mathematics in 1801 at the age of 28, Benjamin Silliman, Professor of Chemistry in 1802 at the age of 23, and James L. Kingsley, Professor of Languages in 1805 at the age of 27. Of these, the first retired from active service in 1846, the second in 1853, and the third in 1851 ; but between the dates of Dr. Dwight's death and their withdrawal, Dr. Dwight lived again in their control of the policy of the institution. The same principle appeared in the brief career of Ebenezer Grant Marsh, in the gift to the Medical School of Eli Ives and Jonathan Knight, and may perhaps also be traced in the promotion after the President's death of such a band of his favorite pupils as Nathaniel W. Taylor, Josiah W. Gibbs, Eleazar T. Fitch, Chauncey A. Goodrich, Alexander M. Fisher, and Denison Olmsted.

Akin to this activity in the discovery of promising talent, was Dr. Dwight's zeal in welcoming the advent of new departments of undergraduate study, and in the expansion of the usefulness of the College by the organization in connection with it of professional schools.

At his entrance on office he found but one Professor in residence, Josiah Meigs, holding the chair of Mathematics on the tenure of annual appointment. Mr. Meigs was an enthusiastic teacher, but indiscreet (in a time of strong party feeling) in expressing his sympathy with the French Revolution and with its American admirers; Dr. Dwight, on the other hand, was equally intense in his devotion to Federalist principles, and such was the general sentiment among the friends of the College. As a result, Mr. Meigs found his position not altogether comfortable, and in 1801 he resigned to accept the Presidency of the University of Georgia. His place was supplied at once by Mr. JEREMIAH DAY'S appointment, and the next year a new chair of Chemistry, Mineralogy, and Geology, the importance of which Dr. Dwight had urged as early as 1798, was established, with Mr. BENJAMIN SILLIMAN as the incumbent. In the same year it was voted to found a Professorship of the Ancient Languages (Hebrew, Greek, and Latin) and Ecclesiastical History,—the last named subject being added as a result of President Stiles's efforts to include it in the curriculum. Mr. Ebenezer Grant Marsh was selected for this post, but being removed by death before his induction, Mr. JAMES L. KINGSLEY was then appointed. Also, in 1801 a Professorship of Law was instituted, with the Hon. ELIZUR GOODRICH, of New Haven, late Member of Congress, as the incumbent, with a small salary; the design was to provide for the Senior Class some general instruction by lectures on the principles of Natural and International Law and on the

Constitution of the United States; Judge Goodrich was obliged by the pressure of other duties to discontinue this service in 1810.

Dr. Dwight's ideal of the College did not stop with the course in Arts, which these Professorships did so much to strengthen. In 1806 the Corporation took the first steps towards founding a MEDICAL DEPARTMENT, to be under their control side by side with the Academical Institution, or Academical Department, as it now began to be called. There was no existing Medical School in the vicinity, and it was thought needful to provide an opportunity for students who wished something superior to the customary training in the family of a village physician. It was eventually thought desirable to establish the new department under the joint auspices of Yale College and the State Medical Society; and an agreement to this effect was approved by the Legislature in 1810. In 1813 Drs. Nathan Smith, Eli Ives, and Jonathan Knight were appointed Professors,—Professor Silliman filling the chair of chemistry, and Dr. Eneas Munson being also nominally associated with the Faculty, though too aged to take any duties. The School began its work in 1813 with 37 students, in the building at the head of College street, which was at first leased, and soon after purchased by means of a grant of $20,000 obtained from the State in 1814, as the result of the personal exertions of Dr. Smith; the same grant furnished the beginning of a library and of an anatomical museum. The first class (of three members) was graduated with the degree of M.D. in 1814.

Prior to this Dr. Dwight had taken deep interest in the establishment of the Theological School in Andover,—the earliest in this country,—and had already entertained the idea of developing a similar school in connection with Yale College. The accomplishment of his plan was made to depend on the success of a business venture of one of his own sons, which had not matured at the time of his death; but it deserves to be noted that Dr. Dwight's plan for the College comprehended a THEOLOGICAL DEPARTMENT, and that he had fixed on the man who was afterwards called to fill the chief chair of instruction. It is also certain that the plan of a LAW DEPARTMENT had entered his mind; he was familiar with the success of Judge Charles Chauncey (from about 1794) and Mr. Seth P. Staples (from about 1800) in the instruction of law students in New Haven, and with the greater success of the Law School in Litchfield, Connecticut; and the recognition of one of these private enterprises as a part of the College in 1824 was the tardy fruition of his policy.

The expansion of the scheme of instruction resulted in a great increase of students (217 in 1800, as against 115 four years before) which required additional College buildings. Accordingly, in 1801 a new dormitory (the present NORTH MIDDLE COLLEGE) and the LYCEUM building (for recitation rooms, a library, and a chemical laboratory) were begun, and both were completed in 1803. The erection of these buildings was due to the Legislative grant of 1792, which had been increased to a total of $40,000 by a supplementary vote in 1796. The President's house (built in 1722) being in a state of decay, a new house for his occupation was erected in 1797–99, on the present site of Farnam College,—the land for all these buildings, and in fact the larger part of the square, having been acquired as early as 1796 by the foresight of Dr. Dwight.

To meet these expenditures, and those required by the enlargement of the corps of instructors, by the marked increase of the Library, and by the purchase of chemical and philosophical apparatus, little beyond what has been named was added to the ordinary resources during Dr. Dwight's administration: the State in 1816 distributed "for the support of literature and religion" certain moneys repaid by the general government for outlays in the recent war, and from this source the College received nearly nine thousand dollars; besides this there was little except a small increase of the Library funds.

President Dwight died in January, 1817, after a year's gradual decline. His administration had been a period of unprecedented prosperity, and under him the College by the increasing number of students from the Southern and Southwestern States had begun to acquire its distinctive character as a NATIONAL INSTITUTION and one in which the UNIVERSITY PRINCIPLE was thenceforth to be recognized. It should not be concealed, however, that his strong political and denominational sympathies were made the occasion, in connection with local controversies, of some opposition to the College, the fruits of which were seen in a movement, which resulted in the charter of Washington (now Trinity) College, in 1823.

President Day's Administration, 1817-46

PRESIDENT DWIGHT had filled so large a space in the public estimation, that it was more than usually difficult to select a successor. The place was first offered to the Rev. HENRY DAVIS, D.D., the President of Middlebury College, who had been a favorite pupil of Dr. Dwight; and on his declining, Professor JEREMIAH DAY was elected. It is understood that Professor Day was Dr. Dwight's own choice for the succession, but his known reluctance to taking the office led to the prior election of another. Professor Day was heartily confided in by his colleagues and former pupils; but beyond these circles, there seemed danger of a decline of prestige for the College in the substitution for so eminent a man as Dr. Dwight of the reserved, unpretentious scholar, who had long been in extremely delicate health, and was only known to the public by a series of mathematical text-books. He had not even the prestige of membership of the clerical profession; but as he had studied theology and had been licensed to preach before his appointment as Professor, and as he viewed the call to the Presidency as involving the same class of obligations as a call to the ministry, he was accordingly ordained at the time of his induction into his new office.

The chair of instruction hitherto held by Presi-

dent Day was filled by the promotion of Mr.
Alexander M. Fisher (Yale 1813), then a tutor.
It also became necessary to supply President
Dwight's place in the chair of Divinity, and to
make good the loss of his instructions in Rhetoric
by the creation of a new chair; to the former
Professorship was appointed (after an unsuccessful
attempt to obtain Dr. Ebenezer Porter, of Andover
Seminary) the Rev. Eleazar T. Fitch (Yale 1810),
and to the latter his classmate, the Rev. Chauncey
A. Goodrich. This enlargement of the Academical Faculty, with the withdrawal of Dr. Dwight's
experienced leadership, caused perhaps unconsciously an increasing reliance on government by
the Faculty and the development of the principle
since accepted as a fixed one in this College, that
in grave matters affecting a Department the Corporation will not take action until the permanent
officers have been expressly consulted, and in particular that the Corporation in filling a Professorship in any Department will await a nomination
from the Professors in that Department.

The growth of the College proper, under the
application of such a system, during the twenty-nine years of President Day's administration, was
sound and symmetrical. His older associates,
Professors Silliman and Kingsley, and also Professor Fitch, continued in full service through this
period; Professor Kingsley's work, however, was
confined to Latin after 1831, when Mr. Theodore
D. Woolsey was appointed Professor of Greek;
and Mr. Thomas A. Thacher was advanced from

a tutorship to an Assistant Professorship of Latin in 1842. The gifted mathematical Professor, Alexander M. Fisher, was lost on a voyage to Europe in 1822; and the Rev. Matthew R. Dutton (Yale 1808) who succeeded to the chair died three years later. Professor Denison Olmsted (Yale 1813), of the University of North Carolina, was then appointed, and in 1836 the chair was divided, —Professor Olmsted devoting himself with marked success to Natural Philosophy and Astronomy, and Mr. Anthony D. Stanley (Yale 1830), then a tutor, being appointed Professor of Mathematics. In 1839 Professor Goodrich was transferred to the Divinity School, and the Rev. William A. Larned (Yale 1826) was made Professor of Rhetoric and English Literature. Dr. Goodrich continued, however, to be in a peculiar sense the religious friend of the students in the College, and by his unofficial pastoral work and impressive personal influence did much to develop the active Christian life of the whole institution.

Great improvements were made in this long period in the course of instruction: some elementary subjects were discarded (as, English Grammar and Geography in 1826, and Arithmetic in 1830), and new subjects, as the modern languages, law, and political economy, introduced; the scope and thoroughness of the examinations for admission were constantly increased; and similar advances made in nearly every subject of College teaching.

Another most important improvement introduced in 1830, through the agency of the Rev. Dr.

Horace Bushnell, then a Tutor, was the abandonment of the system which had up to that date assigned a division of each class to some one of the Tutors, who heard all the recitations in Greek, Latin, and Mathematics, for the current term or year; after 1830 each Tutor confined his instructions to a single subject, instructing in that the divisions of the class in rotation. In 1828 the question of abandoning the required study of the ancient languages came before the Corporation, and an exhaustive report on the subject was prepared by the Faculty. The effect of the discussion may be seen in the emphatic endorsement of the existing system by the division of Professor Kingsley's chair soon after, and the appointment of an enthusiastic young scholar fresh from study in Germany to the sole work of teaching Greek.

The need of additional accommodations for the students received President Day's early attention. In 1818-19 a large DINING HALL was erected, near the center of the College square, of three stories, the kitchen occupying the basement, and the upper floor being devoted to the exhibition of the valuable mineralogical cabinet acquired by Professor Silliman's zeal during the previous decade, while the former Dining Hall was in 1820 devoted to the chemical department; in 1842, however, the system of a common dining hall, which had long been unsatisfactory, was abandoned, and the rooms set free were given over principally to the uses of the department of Natural Philosophy. In 1820-21 the line of brick Colleges was extended by the erection of NORTH COLLEGE, containing like its predecessors 32 rooms, and in 1823-24 a new CHAPEL was built (between North and North Middle Colleges), of which the upper story was divided into rooms for students, while the attic received the Library,—the part of the Lyceum used for that purpose being converted into a rhetorical chamber. In 1831-32 the TRUMBULL GALLERY (now the Treasury Building) was erected, in the rear of the Chapel, to contain the College collection of paintings, especially those by Col. John Trumbull, which were at first deposited by the artist, and later became the property of the College. In 1842 a LIBRARY building of Portland sandstone was begun, on the western side of the square, which was occupied in 1843, though not completed (at a cost of $34,000) before 1846. The Library funds, besides smaller accessions, were substantially increased during this period by the bequest (without conditions) of $3,000 from Mr. Noah Linsly (Yale 1791), of Wheeling, Va., received in 1820-21; by the gift of $5,000 from John T. Norton, Esq., of Albany; and especially by the bequest of $10,000 received in 1836 from the estate of Dr. ALFRED E. PERKINS (Yale 1830), of Norwich, Connecticut; this last was then the largest gift received by the College from any private individual since the days of Governor Yale, and still remains the largest sum contributed to the permanent Library fund from any one source.

Mr. Norton's gift just mentioned was subscribed in connection with an effort undertaken by the alumni in 1831 for a much needed enlargement of the general funds of the College; the sum of $100,000 was thus raised, in 1831-36, of which sum $82,950 was specifically given for the support of the Academical Department. It was true that the State had just made (in 1831) a gift of $7,000 to the College (used in building the Trumbull Gallery), but it seemed vain to expect further State aid, though calls for ampler means were multiplying on every hand. Accordingly, the interest of the alumni was for the first time systematically enlisted in behalf of the needs of their *alma mater*, with this greatly encouraging result; more than three-fourths of the subscriptions were in sums of $100 and less, from graduates and other friends of the College of limited means. The success of this effort was largely due to the agency of the Rev. Wyllys Warner (Yale 1826), who was appointed on the death of the Hon. James Hillhouse in 1832 his successor as Treasurer of the College. The Fund thus collected provided for the establishment of separate chairs of Greek and Mathematics, for the employment of a competent instructor in Elocution, and for relieving a variety of minor pressing necessities.

Few other additions of importance were made to the Academical funds under President Day,— one of the most noteworthy being a bequest of $4,000 in 1835 by Mr. Solomon Langdon, of Farmington, Conn., for the aid of indigent students.

Under Dr. Day there was a tolerably regular increase in the size of the Academical Classes, which averaged at graduation under Dr. Dwight about 56, and under his successor about 90. Among special causes which may have interfered to some extent with larger growth were the foundation of Amherst College in 1821, of Trinity College in 1823, and of Wesleyan University in 1832, and the advance in the terms of admission (as, for instance, the considerable advance made in Greek in 1840).

The foundation of Trinity College was nearly contemporaneous with, if not consequent upon, the organization of a new professional school at Yale. From the creation of the Professorship of Divinity, not to speak of the earlier days, the instruction of graduates in theology had employed a part of the time of Professors Daggett and Wales, and of President Stiles and Dwight. Professor Fitch began the same system, but soon found the pressure on his time and strength too great; so that he was naturally led to suggest to the Corporation, in April, 1822, the appointment of another Professor who should take this as his chief duty. The time proved ripe for the realization of President Dwight's scheme of a THEOLOGICAL DEPARTMENT in the University; and an appeal for the endowment of a chair of Didactic Theology met with such prompt response that the Rev. Nathaniel W. Taylor (Yale 1807) was transfered from the pulpit of the Center Church in New Haven to this office before the end of the year. In his early instructions he was aided by Professors Kingsley, Fitch, and Goodrich; and the two latter were connected with the work for the rest of their active lives, Professor Goodrich in 1839 resigning his Academical chair to devote himself wholly to the Professorship of the Pastoral Charge, for which he furnished an endowment. Professor Kingsley's services were not needed after 1824, when Mr. Josiah W. Gibbs (Yale 1809) was appointed Lecturer on Sacred Literature, his income being partly provided by his undertaking also the duties of College Librarian, previously discharged by Professor Kingsley; in 1826 the Lectureship was changed to a full Professorship; and in 1843 the duties of Librarian were transferred to Mr. Edward C. Herrick. The wonderful power of Dr. Taylor as an instructor attracted many students, so that in 1835-36 a building was erected, in the line of the other College buildings, for the use of the Department.

The MEDICAL SCHOOL was ably conducted under President Day's administration, and for the first ten years with a growing number of students. After that time the establishment of other schools caused a decrease in the attendance here. The death of the most active and most distinguished member of the Faculty, Dr. Smith, in 1829, led to the appointment of three new Professors, Drs. Thomas Hubbard, William Tully, and Timothy P. Beers; on Dr. Hubbard's death in 1838, Dr. Charles Hooker was added to the Faculty, while Dr. Henry Bronson succeeded Dr. Tully in 1841.

The idea of a LAW SCHOOL to be connected with the College had been publicly discussed in

Dr. Dwight's time; and in 1824 the first step was taken towards such a result. In that year Seth P. Staples, Esq. (Yale 1797), who had conducted a flourishing private Law School in New Haven since the beginning of the century, removed to New York, leaving his School in the care of the Hon. David Daggett (Yale 1783) and Samuel J. Hitchcock, Esq. (Yale 1809). Most of the students were Yale graduates; and it was not perhaps an unnatural innovation that their names were in 1824 inserted as "Law Students" in the annual catalogues. This was preparatory to a closer connection, which followed in 1826, when Judge Daggett was appointed to the dormant Professorship of Law (with the duty of occasional lectures to the Academical Seniors), for which a small endowment (named in honor of Chancellor Kent) was now secured. It was not, however, until 1843, that the degree of Bachelor of Laws began to be conferred upon examination, thus placing the Department on an equal footing with that of Medicine. Mr. Hitchcock died in 1845, and was succeeded by the Hon. William L. Storrs (Yale 1814); in 1842 Isaac H. Townsend, Esq. (Yale 1822) also began to give instruction.

Meantime, in 1841, a step of the first importance was taken towards the organization òf GRADUATE INSTRUCTION in lines outside of the three learned professions, by the appointment (without salary) of Mr. Edward E. Salisbury (Yale 1832) as Professor of Arabic and Sanskrit.

PRESIDENT DAY'S long career as head of the

College was terminated by his resignation in 1846, at the age of 73. His health had always been delicate, and once or twice before he had desired to lay down the burdens of office, but had been dissuaded by the representations of those intimately connected with the College. On his resignation he was immediately chosen into the Corporation, and served in that capacity until a few weeks before his decease in 1867. The gravity and calmness which were his striking external characteristics, were in perfect keeping with the whole force of his influence in College affairs. By a well-balanced judgment, cautiousness about changes, regularity and steadiness in the development of matured plans, and other traits similar to these he exercised a great though unobtrusive power, and left a memory for universal veneration.

President Woolsey's Administration, 1846-71

IN the choice of a successor to the Presidency, the policy which had borne such excellent fruits was unhesitatingly followed, and Professor THEODORE DWIGHT WOOLSEY, for fifteen years Professor of Greek, was elected to the office on the day after President Day's resignation was presented. Dr. Woolsey had like his predecessor made in early life a partial preparation for the ministry, and like him, therefore, received ordination at the same time with the induction into the Presidency. He entered on his office in October, 1846, and the progress made in the twenty-five years of his administration was far beyond all precedent in the history of the College.

In the Academical Department one of his earliest duties was the reorganization of the Senior year, which was in part a consequence of the accession to the Faculty in 1847 of the Rev. Noah Porter, in the new Professorship of Moral Philosophy and Metaphysics, founded by the accumulations of a fund given in 1823 by Mr. SHELDON CLARK, a farmer of Oxford, in New Haven County. The improvements lately made in the methods of instruction had affected mainly the three earlier years of the course; and it remained for President Woolsey to bring the Senior year to a corresponding degree of efficiency. His own instructions in history, political science, and international law filled a great part of the year,—Mr. James Hadley being promoted to the charge of the Greek department in 1848; Mr. Lewis R. Packard was advanced from a tutorship to a second chair in the latter department in 1863; while in 1865 the President's duties of instruction were lightened by the creation of a Professorship of History (endowed by Mr. BRADFORD M. C. DURFEE, of Fall River, Mass.), to which Mr. Arthur M. Wheeler was appointed.

Professors Silliman and Kingsley, the lifelong colleagues of President Day, remained for a few years longer than he in active service. In different ways each of the two had impressed himself strongly on the College community. Professor Kingsley, who died in 1852, was the model scholar, keen in appreciation of all scholarly effort, and caustic in reproof of shams; Professor Silliman, who survived until 1864, was the public orator of the College, with a national reputation as an ardent lover of science and a pioneer in its popular exposition.

Geology, before embraced in Professor Silliman's field, was assigned to a distinct Professorship in 1850, to which Mr. James D. Dana (Yale, 1833) was appointed; Mineralogy was added in 1864 to this chair.

The next officer in age, the Rev. Dr. Fitch, a preacher eminent for a brilliant combination of logic and eloquence, resigned the pastorate in 1852, and was succeeded by the Rev. George P. Fisher in 1854, who was transferred in 1861 to the

Divinity School. Two short pastorates followed: the Rev. William B. Clarke's from 1863 to 1866, and the Rev. Dr. Oliver E. Daggett's from 1867 to 1870; in the meantime the foundation for this Professorship was increased by the gifts of the Hon. Simeon B. Chittenden, of Brooklyn, N. Y., to $50,000,—a larger sum than the endowment of any other Academical chair.

Professor Olmsted retained till his death in 1859 the chair of Natural Philosophy and Astronomy, and Professor Stanley the chair of Mathematics until his death in 1853; Mr. Hubert A. Newton succeeded to the latter position in 1855, and Professor Elias Loomis to the former in 1860.

Professor Larned, of the chair of Rhetoric and English Literature, died suddenly in 1862, and Cyrus Northrop, Esq. (Yale, 1857), was appointed his successor.

Another new Professorship belongs to this period:—that of Modern Languages, endowed by Mr. AUGUSTUS R. STREET (Yale, 1812), of New Haven, and filled in 1864 by the appointment of Mr. Edward B. Coe, who began his instructions in 1867; for a long time before this temporary teachers, mostly of foreign birth, had supplied the demands in this direction with varying success, and a trained and permanent head was needed to organize and develop the department; in this connection French was introduced into the curriculum as a required study in the earlier years.

Aside from the changes in the permanent teaching force, a great advance took place under Dr. Woolsey, especially in the latter years of his administration, in the range and quality of the instruction given, and in the amount and character of study required. The influences producing these changes reached their full development in results which belong to the later history, but one or two of early accomplishment may be specified here. Such was the improvement wrought by the introduction of more thorough examinations, as well those for degrees, and for promotion from one year to another, as those for admission. A distinct advantage was gained by subdividing the three lower classes into smaller sections for the purposes of recitation, and by determining these sections by scholarship, not by alphabetical arrangement. A new stimulus was afforded by the creation of special endowments, the income of which was to be used in the way of rewards for the promotion of scholarship; notable among these were four Freshman Scholarships, endowed by the President himself in 1846-48, and a Scholarship, open to Sophomores and Juniors, and tenable for four or five years, which was established by Mr. CHARLES ASTOR BRISTED (Yale, 1839), of New York city, in 1848.

The improvements introduced in the course of instruction, and the changes in prices in the country, necessitated successive advances in the cost of tuition, which had been fixed at $33 in 1811, and was increased in 1852 to $39, in 1856 to $45, in 1866 to $60, and in 1870 to $90.

One incidental adjunct of the increased number and rigor of examinations was the need of a larger hall for such purposes; accordingly a stone building, called ALUMNI HALL, was erected in 1852-53, on the northwest corner of the College square, the lower floor of which was finished in one room, for use in examinations and for general meetings, as those of the Alumni at Commencement, and containing a collection of portraits of officers and benefactors; the upper floor was divided into three halls, for the use of the large literary societies of the College.

The close union of the students in a common life, so striking and valued a feature of the College, was strengthened in this period by the generous gifts of Mr. HENRY FARNAM, of New Haven, and Mr. BRADFORD M. C. DURFEE, of Fall River, Mass., which made possible the erection, in 1869-71, of FARNAM COLLEGE and DURFEE COLLEGE, to accommodate the last of which Divinity College was removed; the old President's house, on the site of Farnam College, had been removed in 1860. These new dormitories, of improved plans, furnished accommodation for 169 persons. In this connection a steam boiler-house was constructed, from which most of the buildings on the College square and in the vicinity are heated.

Another great addition to the square was the erection, in 1864-66, on the Southwest corner, by Mr. AUGUSTUS R. STREET (Yale 1812), of an elegant building for the accommodation of the SCHOOL OF THE FINE ARTS, two of the Professorships in which also received endowments from Mr. and Mrs. Street. The School thus endowed, and designed in the intention of the founder to form an important adjunct to the Undergraduate instruction, was opened to students in 1869, when Mr. John F. Weir, N. A., was appointed Professor of Painting, and Director of the School, and D. Cady Eaton, Esq., was elected to a Professorship of the History of Art. After the erection of the Art School, the paintings deposited by Colonel Trumbull in the Trumbull Gallery were transferred thither, and the latter building was devoted (from 1868) to a President's office and the ampler accommodation of the Treasury. Mr. Warner had retired from the office of Treasurer in 1852, and had been succeeded by Mr. Edward C. Herrick, at whose death in 1862, Mr. Henry C. Kingsley was appointed.

On one of the adjoining squares on the west, a Gymnasium for the use of the Academical Department was erected in 1859.

The chief addition to the resources of the College under President Woolsey, besides those named, was the "FUND OF 1854," collected by a general subscription, and amounting to $106,390, of which about $70,000 was devoted by the subscribers to the general needs of the Academical Department. This relief enabled the Corporation among other things to meet the expense of a rise in the annual salaries of the Academical Professors, which had remained substantially unchanged since 1817, when they were fixed at $1,100.

The LIBRARY funds received some additions, the most considerable being the sum of $5,000, the accumulations of a legacy bequeathed in 1842 by Addin Lewis, Esq. (Yale, 1803), of New Haven, but not received until 1849. The Library was also enriched by many large gifts of books, conspicuously by the presentation in 1869 of the extremely valuable Oriental library collected by Professor Salisbury, who supplemented this gift with a provision for additions to the collection, thus rendering this important department among the most complete in the Library. Mr. Herrick resigned the Librarianship in 1858, and was succeeded by Mr. Daniel C. Gilman, who had already for two years acted as his Assistant. On Mr. Gilman's retirement in 1865, Mr. Addison Van Name, who still holds the position, was appointed. In 1867 Mr. Franklin B. Dexter was put in charge of the construction of a new card-catalogue, and in 1869 he was permanently connected with the Library, as Assistant Librarian.

Of the other Departments, the DIVINITY SCHOOL under President Woolsey entered on a new career of prosperity. Of the Faculty who had given it its early reputation, Dr. Taylor died in 1858, Professor Goodrich in 1860, and Professor Gibbs in 1861, in which year also Dr. Fitch's name disappeared from the list of instructors. A new era for the Seminary began with the appointment in 1858 of Mr. Timothy Dwight (Yale 1849), as Assistant Professor of Sacred Literature. With him was associated in the work of reconstruction, in

1861, as Professor of Ecclesiastical History, the Rev. George P. Fisher, transferred from the College pastorate; and the same year was marked by the accession of the Rev. James M. Hoppin to the chair of Homiletics, and of Mr. Henry H. Hadley to the chair of Hebrew; Mr. Hadley remained but a single year, and his place was supplied by Mr. Addison Van Name, until the appointment of Professor George E. Day in 1866. In 1866 the Faculty was further strengthened by the addition of the Rev. Dr. Leonard Bacon, who on his retirement from active duty as pastor of the First Church of New Haven, assumed a part of the instruction in Theology in the Seminary, which had been assigned since Dr. Taylor's death to Professor Porter of the Academical Department. These temporary arrangements continued until 1871, when the Rev. Dr. Samuel Harris, President of Bowdoin College, accepted the Professorship of Systematic Theology; Dr. Bacon continued to give valuable service in the Faculty as Lecturer on Church Polity and American Church History until his death in 1881.

Just after Governor WILLIAM A. BUCKINGHAM had contributed $25,000 to the funds for instruction, the death of that munificent friend of the University, Mr. AUGUSTUS R. STREET, in 1866, provided an endowment of nearly $50,000 for the chair of Ecclesiastical History; and the wise step taken the same year, of recognizing the relation of this Department to the University by entitling its future graduates to the degree of BACHELOR OF

DIVINITY, insured permanent success to the work which was next undertaken.

In the prospect that the site of the Divinity College erected thirty years before would soon be demanded by the Academical Department for its needs, subscriptions were opened in 1866 for a new Hall, and by the devoted efforts of the Faculty for this object funds to the amount of $133,000 were secured, and a handsome building (EAST DIVINITY HALL) erected in 1869–70 on the square next north of the College. In connection with this a fund for an excellent Reference Library was contributed by Henry Trowbridge, Esq., of New Haven. The Chapel adjoining this building, the gift of Frederick Marquand, Esq., of Southport, Connecticut, was added in 1871.

The corps of instruction was enlarged in 1871 by means of the gift of $10,000 from Henry W. Sage, Esq., of Brooklyn, N. Y., for the foundation of a lectureship on Preaching and other appropriate topics, to be filled from year to year by the appointment of distinguished pastors of any denomination,—a provision of great advantage to the students. Other important additions were made to the scholarship and general funds.

These external improvements were accompanied with a satisfactory growth in numbers of students.

The oldest professional School, that of Medicine, underwent in Dr. Woolsey's administration, like the Divinity School, an entire reconstruction of its Faculty. Of the original staff, Professor Silliman and Dr. Ives continued in active service until

1853, and Dr. Knight until 1864; the next in rank, Dr. Beers, retired in 1856; Dr. Charles Hooker died in 1863, and Dr. Bronson resigned in 1860. Dr. Worthington Hooker was added to the Faculty in 1852, and died in 1867, being succeeded by Dr. Charles L. Ives; Professor Benjamin Silliman, Jr. took his father's place in 1853; Dr. Pliny A. Jewett served as Professor from 1856 until 1864, when he was succeeded by Dr. Stephen G. Hubbard; Dr. Charles A. Lindsley became Professor in 1860, Dr. Leonard J. Sanford in 1863, Dr. Francis Bacon in 1864, and Dr. Moses C. White and George F. Barker in 1867.

An important event in this period was the sale of the building and grounds in 1859, and the erection of a new Medical College, on York street, in 1860. In the later years, the constant and self-denying efforts of the Faculty, who were nearly all engaged in professional practice, were directed to the lengthening and making more thorough the course of study. The lack of pecuniary endowments embarrassed, however, all their plans.

The LAW SCHOOL at President Woolsey's accession was under the charge of Judge Daggett, then extremely aged, and of Judge Storrs,—both of whom retired in 1847,—and of Mr. Townsend who died in the same year. A new Faculty was then appointed, consisting of Governor Clark Bissell and the Hon. Henry Dutton. Governor Bissell retired in 1855, and his successor, the Hon. Thomas B. Osborne, assisted Professor Dutton for ten years longer. Judge Dutton was then left in sole charge until his death in 1869, the attendance meantime having seriously fallen off. A new departure was then taken, which subsequently under President Woolsey's successor amounted to a reconstruction of the School.

Before 1846, plans were under weigh for the establishment of a DEPARTMENT OF (non-professional) GRADUATE INSTRUCTION. A distinct impulse had been given in this direction by Professor Salisbury's appointment in 1841, and by the instruction of advanced students in chemistry and natural history in Professor Silliman's laboratory. In August, 1846, the important step was taken of constituting two new Professorships,—one of Agricultural Chemistry, for which a small endowment was partially promised, and one of Practical or Applied Chemistry,—and the arrangement of a scheme for organized graduate instruction, which should include the entire work of these chairs, was begun. Messrs. John P. Norton and Benjamin Silliman, Jr., were appointed to the new professorships, and in August, 1847, the courses of graduate study which were or might be provided (apart from those embraced in the Theological, Medical and Law Schools) were recognized as forming the " DEPARTMENT OF PHILOSOPHY AND THE ARTS." Various new courses in Philology, Philosophy, and Science, were at once announced by other Professors, for combination with the courses offered by Professors Salisbury, Silliman, Jr., and Norton, and a chemical laboratory was opened in the building long used as a President's House, which Dr. Woolsey did not desire to occupy.

In 1852 the degree of BACHELOR OF PHILOSOPHY was first given to members of the Department who had satisfactorily completed a two-years' course covering at least three branches of study. In the same year Professor Norton, a most promising scholar, was removed by death at the age of thirty. His place was supplied (at first *pro tempore*) by Professor John A. Porter. In 1852 a chair of civil engineering was also established, with Professor William A. Norton as incumbent.

In 1854 the side of philological science was greatly strengthened by the creation of a separate Professorship of Sanskrit (hitherto included in Professor Salisbury's chair), to which Mr. William D. Whitney was appointed; and in the same year the instruction in chemistry and engineering began to be distinguished as a separate section of the Department, with the title of the "YALE SCIENTIFIC SCHOOL." A year later another chair, that of Metallurgy, was added to this section, with Mr. George J. Brush, one of the earliest graduates of the Department, as Professor; and in 1856 the Chemical courses were further reinforced by the appointment of Mr. Samuel W. Johnson as Professor, to whom Agricultural and Analytical Chemistry were afterwards assigned, Professor Porter retaining Organic Chemistry until his retirement from ill-health in 1864.

The Scientific School grew rapidly, despite the lack of endowments and the poor accommodations afforded in the old President's House and the attic of the Chapel. In 1859, a generous friend,

JOSEPH E. SHEFFIELD, Esq., of New Haven, purchased and enlarged for the use of the School the former Medical College, stocked it with appropriate apparatus, and gave a fund of $50,000 for the endowment of Professorships. In recognition of this generosity, the Corporation in 1860 applied the name of the SHEFFIELD SCIENTIFIC SCHOOL to this section of the Philosophical Department. Meantime, in 1859, an additional chair, of Industrial Mechanics and Physics, had been filled by the appointment of the Rev. Chester S. Lyman.

The next step was the Act of the State Legislature in 1863, appropriating to this school the income from the fund of $135,000 realized by the sale of lands assigned to Connecticut by the Act of Congress in 1862, which donated public lands to those States which should provide Colleges for the benefit of Agriculture and the Mechanic Arts. As a condition of this grant, a certain number (in proportion to the income) of scholars living in Connecticut receive free tuition annually. From this date the excellence of the instruction furnished and the new openings in this country for scientific men increased beyond expectation the numbers of the students, and this led to rapid enlargements of the facilities offered. In 1863 Mr. Daniel C. Gilman was added to the Faculty (or Governing Board, as it soon began to be called), as Professor of Physical and Political Geography; in 1864 Professor William H. Brewer was appointed to a chair of Agriculture, and Mr. Addison E. Verrill to a chair of Zoology. In the same year also

Mr. Daniel C. Eaton was made Professor of Botany in the general Philosophical Department, and identified himself specially with the Sheffield School. In 1865 Col. Alfred P. Rockwell was made Professor of Mining, but resigned the position in 1868. In 1865 the school-building (called SHEFFIELD HALL) was greatly enlarged at Mr. Sheffield's expense, making his outlay in this direction alone about $150,000, besides a library fund of $10,000. The same year, the term of study for the degree of Bachelor of Philosophy was extended from two years to three, the degree of CIVIL ENGINEER having been already offered as early as 1860 to those taking an additional year of engineering study. The degree of DOCTOR OF PHILOSOPHY had also been established in 1860, in the general Department, to be given after two years' advanced study to those graduates of the Bachelor's degree who had previously made attainments substantially equivalent in amount to those covered by the four years' undergraduate course in the College. In this connection it should also be stated that the number of distinct undergraduate courses of study in the Sheffield School was gradually enlarged in this period from the two earliest (in Chemistry and Engineering) to seven, namely, in Chemistry and Metallurgy, in Civil Engineering, in Dynamical or Mechanical Engineering, in Agriculture, in Natural History, in Biology preparatory to Medical studies, in studies preparatory to Mining, and in Select studies preparatory to other pursuits, to business, etc. The course in Dynamical Engineering was amplified in 1870, when Captain William P. Trowbridge was appointed to a Professorship with that title, which was endowed in 1871 to the amount of $28,000, by Mrs. SUSAN K. HIGGIN, of Liverpool, England. This gift was in connection with an effort begun in 1869 for the raising of endowments, which resulted in less than three years to the addition of over $150,000 to the permanent fund; of this sum full one-half was contributed by Mr. Sheffield, who was also engaged during these years in the erection of a second building for the school (NORTH SHEFFIELD HALL), at an expense of $115,000, besides the land. The increase of funds also allowed of the appointment (in 1871) of two new Professors,—Mr. Thomas R. Lounsbury to a chair of English, and Mr. Oscar D. Allen to a chair of Metallurgy.

The rapid development thus sketched of the Sheffield School affected both the undergraduate students, candidates for the degree of Bachelor of Philosophy, and the graduate section, or candidates for the degrees of Civil Engineer and Doctor of Philosophy. Meantime the other courses of graduate study (not included in the programme of the Scientific School) were steadily maintained by Professor Whitney and the Academical Professors. Professor Salisbury retired from the chair of Arabic in 1856, but his continued interest in the efficiency of the Department was shown by his endowment (completed in 1870) of the Sanskrit Professorship with a fund of $50,000.

A Professorship of Palæontology, with Mr.

Othniel C. Marsh as incumbent, was added in 1866; and in the same year Mr. GEORGE PEABODY, of London, committed to a Board of Trustees the sum of $150,000, " to found and maintain a MUSEUM OF NATURAL HISTORY, especially in the departments of Zoology, Geology, and Mineralogy, in connection with Yale College."

At the close of President Woolsey's administration an important change was effected in the composition of the Corporation. By request of that body, in response to a general sentiment among the alumni, which Dr. Woolsey favored, the General Assembly of Connecticut passed an Act, in July, 1871, consenting to the substitution of six of the graduates of the College for the six senior senators of the State in the membership of the Corporation. The change was welcomed, as giving the graduates a more direct interest in the administration of the College, while it was acknowledged that the State senators had not in recent years rendered any valuable service as Fellows. The new scheme provided for a six-years' term of office, with one place to be filled each year at Commencement.

President Porter's Administration, 1871-86

DR. WOOLSEY resigned in the summer of 1871, at the age of 70, and his place was filled without delay by the promotion of Professor NOAH PORTER, who had occupied the chair of Moral Philosophy and Metaphysics since 1846.

Dr. Porter's presidency extended for fifteen years, or till July, 1886—a period of steady growth.

Most notable, perhaps, in this period, was the creation of a body of funds for University uses, the impulse to which was furnished by the proposal at the time of President Woolsey's resignation to raise by subscription a permanent fund, which should be called by his name, and the income of which should be available for the benefit of the various departments, in common, or at discretion; about $168,000 was realized from this effort. Other funds of a nearly equal amount, received by the Corporation in these years, without restrictions, were set apart to a like use.

This action was accompanied by a continued increase of the facilities for advanced instruction, and by a recognition (in 1872) of the University principles, in the consolidation under the name of the DEPARTMENT OF PHILOSOPHY AND THE ARTS of all the courses, both graduate and undergraduate, not included in the Departments of Theology, Medicine, and Law.

This period was also marked by the striking

increase (from 7 to 17) in foundations for the maintenance of graduate scholars (of the Academical Department) pursuing non-professional studies. Further to encourage such work, the conditions of bestowing the degree of MASTER OF ARTS (hitherto given as a matter of course) were changed in 1874, so as to require an examination after a year's liberal study.

In the ACADEMICAL DEPARTMENT the revision of the course of instruction and the increase of the teaching force most deserve notice. The Faculty were authorized as early as 1874 to add the elements of a modern language (French or German) to the requirements of admission, though this change was not fully put into operation at once; other alterations in the terms of admission were in the line of previous changes.

The elective system had long been applied in a limited way to a part of the studies of the Junior year; and in 1876 by an extension of the principle nearly one-half of the work of the last two years was left to be determined by each student for himself, the choice being made from a large number of elective courses open to him. In 1884 a further extension of the system took place, by which a little over one-half of the work of the Junior year, and four fifths of the work of the Senior year were given up to elective courses.

The provision of these courses in sufficient fullness would not have been possible, had not the increase of the teaching force kept pace to some extent with the new demands. A chair of Mathematical Physics (Professor J. Willard Gibbs) was established in 1871, and at the same date the ancient chair of Chemistry was again filled, with the addition of Molecular Physics to the department (Professor Arthur W. Wright); in 1872 chairs of German (Professor Franklin Carter) and of Political and Social Science (Professor William G. Sumner) were founded; in 1877 a chair of American History (Professor Franklin B. Dexter); in 1880 an additional chair of Latin (Professor Tracy Peck); and in 1881 the long vacant chair of Law (Hon. Edward J. Phelps) and an additional chair of Mental Philosophy (Professor George T. Ladd) were filled. Besides these, the department of Mathematics was strengthened by the permanent retention of Messrs. Eugene L. Richards (from 1871) and Andrew W. Phillips (from 1881), at first appointed to terminable Assistant Professorships; in the same way Professor Henry P. Wright was added (1871) to the staff in Latin, Professor Henry A. Beers (1874) to the department of English Literature, and Professor Edward S. Dana (1879) to that of Natural Philosophy. The appointment of Assistant Professors in Greek and in the Modern Languages made those departments also more effective.

Professor Thomas A. Thacher died in April, 1886, after 47 years of self-sacrificing service, not the least memorable of which lay outside the class-room, in his influence among the students, his interest in the graduates and his earnest devotion to all measures for the progress of the College.

The Greek Department also lost by death in 1872 that profound and versatile scholar, Professor Hadley, and again in 1884 his colleague, Professor Packard; to the vacancy caused by Professor Hadley's death and by the resignation of Professor Frederic D. Allen (first named as his successor), Professor Thomas D. Seymour was appointed in 1880.

Other changes were the following:—Professor Northrop accepted in 1884 the Presidency of the University of Minnesota, and Professor Carter in 1881 the Presidency of Williams College; Professor Coe resigned in 1879, to enter the ministry, and his chair was filled by the election of Professor William I. Knapp. The Professorship of Divinity (or College pastorate) was filled in 1877 by the appointment of the Rev. Dr. William M. Barbour, of Bangor Theological Seminary.

The funds of the Academical Department received many additions in this time, the largest item being the gift of Dr. T. Dwight Porter (Yale 1816), in 1878-80, amounting to about $115,000, not however all productive; the main part of the income of this sum (after an annuity to his daughter) was appropriated to the increase and support of the teaching force. Another large gift, amounting to upwards of $86,000, was received from the estate of Henry T. Morgan, Esq., of New York City, without conditions; the donor's known wishes were respected by appropriating the income to the remission of tuition for needy and deserving students. Another gift which was first available for use in 1876 was a bequest (now amounting to $56,000) from the Hon. Henry L. Ellsworth (Yale 1810), who died in 1858, the income of which was designed for the assistance of indigent students preparing for the ministry and is thus distributed in the College and in the Divinity School. Other gifts received were mainly in the way of endowments for instruction or for the promotion of scholarship.

Important additions were made to the buildings of the College in this period. A new Chapel was erected on the northeast corner of the College Square in 1874-76, and received the name of BATTELL CHAPEL, in honor of Joseph Battell, Esq., of New York City, from whose gifts the chief part of the expense was defrayed, and also in honor of the generous benefactions of other members of the same family. The old Chapel was rearranged at this time so as to provide seven much needed recitation-rooms.

In 1882-83 a PHYSICAL LABORATORY, most admirably adapted for its purpose, was erected on the south side of Library street and equipped for use by Messrs. HENRY T. and THOMAS C. SLOANE (Yale 1866 and 1868), of New York City, as a memorial to their father. In 1885-86 another dormitory was built on the College square, next Farnam College on the south, containing forty-two suites of rooms, and of five stories in height; the name of LAWRANCE COLLEGE was given to it, in memory of Thomas Garner Lawrance, of New York City, a member of the Class of 1884, who died in his Senior year, and whose mother's gift of $50,000 was appropriated to this purpose. In the same years a beautifully furnished building, called DWIGHT HALL, in memory of President Dwight, was erected north of the Library, at the expense of ELBERT B. MONROE, Esq., of New York City, to provide an attractive center for the religious life of the College, by a reading-room, select library, and rooms for class-meetings and general meetings.

Another building of the utmost importance to the College, and equally so to all the departments, was the initial portion of the PEABODY MUSEUM of Natural History, which was erected from a portion of Mr. Peabody's munificent endowment, at a cost of $100,000, on High street facing Alumni Hall. The large collections in palaeontology and zoology made by Professors Marsh and Verrill thus became available for exhibition and study, while the College cabinet of mineralogical and geological specimens was also removed to the Museum, and the space thus vacated was utilized for a Reading-Room, previously accommodated but poorly in one of the older buildings.

Another adjunct of the University which took form during these years was an OBSERVATORY for astronomical and physical researches, for which a site had been given by Mrs. Cornelia L. Hillhouse and daughters, in 1858, on Prospect street, about a mile and a quarter north from the College square. In 1871-72 additional ground adjoining this site was purchased at a cost of $100,000 by the Hon.

OLIVER F. WINCHESTER, of New Haven, and in 1879 this was presented to the College, with the expectation that a fund would be realized sufficient for the foundation and maintenance of an Observatory by the gradual sale of portions of the land thus given. A beginning was at once made, chiefly in the direction of organizing a standard time service, and in 1882 a portion of the proposed Observatory buildings was erected, and an equatorial telescope and a valuable heliometer added to the instruments on hand.

The COLLEGE LIBRARY during the same period continued its steady growth. Its fund was increased more than fifty per cent. (from $32,000 to $55,000), though no larger single gift for that purpose was received than the bequest of $5,000 from Mrs. Irene (Battell) Larned in 1877; it should be noted also that after 1874 the Library had the benefit of the income of a fund of $50,000, which was left by JOHN JAY PHELPS, Esq., of New York City, in trust for the College, his son and executor, the Hon. William Walter Phelps, having the power to distribute the income during his life.

A change of great value was accomplished in 1871–72, when the libraries belonging to the LINONIAN SOCIETY and the BROTHERS IN UNITY (student organizations, founded respectively in 1753 and 1768), which had since the erection of the Library building occupied its two wings, were transferred to the care of the College Library, consolidated in one room, and made immeasurably more useful than ever before as the collection of general literature which the undergraduate students most especially consult.

For the SHEFFIELD SCIENTIFIC SCHOOL this period was one of marked prosperity, while the number of students was nearly doubled. The most important advance was the institution in 1873 of the degree of DYNAMIC or MECHANICAL ENGINEER, to be given on a two-years' course of study after graduation as Bachelor of Philosophy; and the similar lengthening at the same time of the course for the degree of CIVIL ENGINEER.

Five new Professorships were created in the period under review:—of Mathematics in 1873 (Professor John E. Clark), of Chemistry (Professor William G. Mixter), and Comparative Anatomy (Professor Sidney I. Smith) in 1875; of Physiological Chemistry (Professor Russell H. Chittenden) in 1882; and of Physics (Professor Charles S. Hastings) in 1884.

Professor Gilman was called to the Presidency of the University of California in 1872, and in his stead Gen. Francis A. Walker was elected Professor of Political Economy and History. Professor Gilman had also, as Secretary of the School, been its principal executive officer; on his removal Professor Brush succeeded to this duty, and was subsequently recognized by the action of the Corporation as the Director of the School and the responsible head of its greatly enlarged organization.

Professor Walker resigned in 1880, to assume the Presidency of the Massachusetts Institute of Technology, and his place in the department of

Political Economy was filled by the election of Mr. Henry W. Farnam. Professor Trowbridge resigned in 1877, to accept a professorship in Columbia College, and was succeeded by Professor A. Jay DuBois. Professor William A. Norton, the senior officer in the School, died in 1883, and in 1884 Professor DuBois was transferred to the chair of Civil Engineering, while Mr. Charles B. Richards was appointed Professor of Mechanical Engineering.

Mr. SHEFFIELD, the munificent patron of the School, having witnessed in his lifetime such wonderful progress in the realization of his benevolent purposes, died in 1882, and by the terms of his will the School received large additions to its funds, which have not yet fully matured.

During the early part of Dr. Porter's administration the ART SCHOOL was occupied in developing its plan of work. Mr. John H. Niemeyer was added to the Faculty as Professor of Drawing in 1871, and the place of Professor Eaton (who resigned in 1876) was filled by the appointment of Professor James M. Hoppin in 1879. Courses of technical instruction in the various arts of design were provided, to which students of both sexes were admitted,—this being the only section of the University in which the arrangements made admit of women being received as pupils. There was also a constant endeavor, by lectures and other optional courses of study, to carry out the intention of the founder and make this School an important factor in the aesthetic development of the undergraduate students in the College. A valuable collection of paintings, both ancient and modern, and of casts from the antique, was accumulated, to aid in the work of instruction. The DIVINITY SCHOOL shared in the general prosperity of the period under consideration. The suite of buildings begun in 1869 was completed by the erection of a second (or WEST) DIVINITY HALL in 1873-74, and a building (named the Bacon Memorial Library, in honor of the Rev. Dr. Bacon) for the Reference LIBRARY in 1881. Donations to the funds for instruction made it possible in 1880 to institute a more thorough course in Elocution, and in 1885 to add to the Faculty a Professor of Biblical Theology (Rev. John E. Russell). In 1876 the first endowment was received for a graduate fellowship, which was established as a memorial of the late Mrs. Aurelia D. Hooker, of New Haven; and three years later full provision was made for the instruction of a class of graduates, who should desire to continue their studies for a fourth year. The expansion of the regular course of study also provided, as a special feature, for the delivery of numerous lectures by eminent preachers and teachers from abroad. Professor Hoppin retired from the chair of Pastoral Theology in 1879, and after an interval, in which instruction was supplied by Professor Barbour, the Rev. Dr. Lewis O. Brastow was appointed to the vacancy in 1885.

The largest donor to the improvements named was Mr. FREDERICK MARQUAND, previously a distinguished benefactor, who now bore half the cost of the site and construction of West Divinity Hall (in all $160,000) and the entire expense of the new Library building, and also furnished half the amount of the fund for Elocution (in all $10,000). Next in value to Mr. Marquand's gifts were a gift of $50,000 from Mr. HENRY WINKLEY, of Philadelphia, for the endowment of the chair of Biblical Theology, and a legacy of $25,000 from ASA OTIS, Esq., of New London, Connecticut, to the general fund.

The LAW SCHOOL in this period underwent a thorough reorganization, and for the first time reached a condition of permanent efficiency, worthy of the University. After Judge Dutton's death in 1869, three members of the New Haven Bar, Messrs. William C. Robinson, Simeon E. Baldwin, and Johnson T. Platt, were put in charge of the School, and in 1872 the same gentlemen, with the Hon. Francis Wayland, were appointed Professors in full, gratifying success having already been attained under their instructions. In 1872 the School was provided with spacious apartments in the new County Court House, and within a short time about $25,000 was subscribed by friends and expended in the purchase of books for the Library, which also received a permanent fund of $10,000 from the Hon. JAMES E. ENGLISH, of New Haven. A comprehensive two-years' course of study was arranged under the new Faculty, with a required examination for admission (after 1875) and annual examinations in writing (after 1873); many special courses of lectures were also introduced.

In 1876 an advanced course in law and political science for graduates was provided, with the offer of the degree of Master of Laws after one year's study, and that of Doctor of Civil Law after two years' study. A chair of International Law was established in 1878, with Mr. Theodore S. Woolsey, who had given instruction in this subject since 1876, as incumbent; and in 1881 a chair of Pleading was added, with William K. Townsend, Esq., as Professor.

Besides the English Fund and some small funds for prizes, one other prospective endowment belongs to this period: the Hon. LAFAYETTE S. FOSTER, who had been a lecturer in the School, left by will in 1880 the sum of $60,000 (subject to a life-interest) for founding a Professorship of Common Law.

In the MEDICAL SCHOOL important improvements were made in the lecture-rooms and laboratories, and a reorganization of the course was effected in 1879, so as to exact three full years of graded study, with examinations in writing. It was hoped that the additional expense entailed by this step, and especially by the development of the instruction in Chemistry, Histology, Physiology, and Pathology, would be met by new endowments, if not by an increase in the numbers of students.

A gift of $5,000 to the general fund of the

School was received in 1877 from John DeForest, M.D., of Watertown, Connecticut, a generous benefactor in other ways of the University.

Of the Faculty, Drs. Ives and Barker resigned in 1873, Dr. Bacon in 1877, and Dr. Hubbard in 1880. Dr. David P. Smith, of Springfield, Mass., was elected to a Professorship in 1873, and died in 1880, to the great loss of the University; by his will his valuable professional library and instruments were given to the School, and provision was made for the ultimate endowment of one of the chairs of instruction. Dr. Lucian S. Wilcox, of Hartford, was added to the Faculty in 1877, but died in 1881; Professor Silliman, the Senior officer in the Faculty, died in 1885. Other appointments were:—Drs. William H. Carmalt and James K. Thacher in 1879; Dr. Frank E. Beckwith in 1880; Dr. Thomas H. Russell in 1883; Dr. Herbert E. Smith in 1885; and Dr. James Campbell in 1886.

In exemplification of the growth of facilities for advanced instruction referred to on page 81, it should especially be stated that, just at the close of President Porter's administration, two notable appointments were made in the Graduate section of the Department of Philosophy and the Arts; that of Mr. Arthur T. Hadley, as Professor of Political Science, and that of Dr. William R. Harper, as Professor of the Semitic Languages.

The University in 1886-87

IN October, 1885, Dr. Porter signified his intention of resigning the Presidency at the close of the current College year; and in view of this intention Professor Timothy Dwight, of the Divinity School, a grandson of the former President Dwight, was elected in May as his successor. He was inducted into office on July 1, 1886, and began his active duties with the assembling of College in September.

After President Dwight's accession the Corporation officially authorized the use of the term University in describing the institution, which though still a College in legal name had in fact become a University by the organization and development of the various departments and courses of instruction. This step was in accord with the President's expressed conception of the immediate future as a period of progress in the line of the University idea. An Act of the General Assembly of the State in March, 1887, authorized the use of the new name as equally legal with the former corporate designation.

Few striking changes have marked President Dwight's first year of office. Mr. Henry C. Kingsley, after having served as Treasurer for nearly 25 years, was removed by a sudden death in December, 1886. His wise and prudent management of the invested funds had been an important factor in their growth, from less than seven hundred thousand dollars in 1862, when he took office, to considerably over two millions in 1886.

A gift of $75,000 from Mr. Albert E. Kent, of Chicago, of the Class of 1853, for a new CHEMICAL LABORATORY for the College, was received before President Dwight's accession, but the erection of the building, on High Street opposite the Library, was postponed until 1887. In anticipation of this building, an additional Professor of Chemistry has been appointed, Dr. Frank A. Gooch. In 1887 a gift of $100,000 was offered by the Hon. Simeon B. Chittenden, of Brooklyn, N. Y., for a much needed enlargement of the University Library; it is expected that the present year will see this structure begun, and that a separate portion of the building, the architecture and decoration of which will be specially cared for, will be an ample reading-room, which will also be a special memorial of a deceased daughter of the donor.

Another gift, of $25,000, has been offered and accepted in 1887 for the endowment of instruction in the Law School by an unknown donor through the Hon. Edward J. Phelps, the Professor of Law in the College. In 1887 arrangements have been completed for offering in the Law School the degree of Bachelor of Civil Law to students who have pursued here a two years' course which is especially designed to give a general knowledge of the principles of legal and political science, but not necessarily leading to a professional career.

THE spirit and tendency of the new administration cannot be judged by the few incidents thus outlined, occurring within the first months of its progress. It is more just to refer to the deliberate utterances of President Dwight, at his induction into office, when he expressed his hope of representing the University idea as connected with that of the original College, and so of accomplishing something for the healthful development of the future. With this aim on the part of the government, and the hearty sympathy and support of the graduates and friends of the University, a period of useful expansion in the immediate future may be anticipated, under the general principles which have been the basis of administration in the past.

Diu floreat Alma Mater Yalensis!

APPENDIX,

Statistical and Bibliographical

The present PRESIDENT is the twelfth holder of the office, the average term of service of his predecessors being 16½ years,—ranging from the 3½ years of Rector Cutler to the 29 years of President Day.

The average term of office of the clerical TRUSTEES or FELLOWS who have completed their service (105 in all) is 16.7 years; that of the Alumni Fellows who are no longer in office is 8.8 years. The longest term of service in the Corporation is that of President Day, who was 29 years President, and 21 years Fellow,—50 years in all; next to his name is that of the Rev. David Smith, D.D., a Fellow for 40 years (1821–61).

The first Professor was appointed in 1755, and since that date 132 persons have occupied the position. The average length of the completed terms of active service is 17.4 years; the longest in service were Benjamin Silliman, Senior, and Jonathan Knight, each 51 years. Next to these is James L. Kingsley, who was in continuous service (including his tutorship) for 50 years. President Day was connected with the institution continuously, as Tutor, Professor, President and Fellow, for 69 years,—a longer period than is recorded of any other individual.

The average length of life of the Presidents and Professors who have died in office, or have ended their active careers with their retirement from office here, is 64 years.

The earliest CATALOGUE of the GRADUATES was printed, with the graduating theses for that year, in 1714; a similar broadside appeared in 1718; and in 1724 the first independent Catalogue of Graduates appeared. Successive editions have appeared triennially from that date until 1886; they were on single folio sheets until 1781, when the octavo form was adopted.

The Annual CATALOGUES of STUDENTS begin with the issue of 1796, on a broadside; though occasional lists of single classes had been issued for twenty-five years earlier. The first of the Annual Catalogues in pamphlet form (octavo) appeared in 1813; they contained merely lists of the officers and students until 1822, when a Statement of the Course of Instruction, Expenses, etc., was added.

The FAMILY NAMES most largely represented in the last catalogue (1886) of the Graduates of the University are the following: Smith or Smyth, 203; Williams, 108; Clark or Clarke, 103; Brown or Browne, 80; Hall, 79; Baldwin, 67; Hubbard, 66; Strong, 66; Johnson, 61; Adams, 54; Huntington, 54; Jones, 53.

The first graduating class which numbered more than 50 persons was the Class of 1777; not until 1826 did the number of the Bachelors of Arts for any year reach 100; and the largest class of B.A.'s thus far is the Class of 1884 (150).

Appendix

Number of Graduates

	B.A.	M.D.	LL.B.	Ph.B.	C.E.	Ph.D.	B.D.	M.E.	M.A. (on exam)	M.L.	D.C.L.
1702–1716 (at Saybrook),	56	--	--	--	--	--	--	--	--	--	--
Yearly average,	3.7										
1717–1739 (Rectors Andrew, Cutler, Williams),	330	--	--	--	--	--	--	--	--	--	--
Yearly average,	14.4										
1740–1766 (President Clap),	757	--	--	--	--	--	--	--	--	--	--
Yearly average,	28										
1767–1777 (President Daggett),	330	--	--	--	--	--	--	--	--	--	--
Yearly average,	30										
1778–1795 (President Stiles),	669	--	--	--	--	--	--	--	--	--	--
Yearly average,	37.1										
1796–1817 (President Dwight),	1137	32	--	--	--	--	--	--	--	--	--
Yearly average,	51.7	8									
1818–1846 (President Day),	2308	519	25	--	--	--	--	--	--	--	--
Yearly average,	79.6	17.9	6.3								
1847–1871 (President Woolsey),	2559	314	184	233	9	20	30	--	--	--	--
Yearly average,	102.4	12.6	7.4	11.7	.7	1.8	6				
1872–1886 (President Porter),	1874	127	387	671	19	60	378	10	28	33	8
Yearly average,	124.9	8.5	25.8	44.7	1.3	4	25.2	.7	2.5	3.3	.9
TOTAL,	10020	992	596	904	28	80	408	10	28	33	8

The average AGE OF ADMISSION to College in the first half-century was about 17 years. In the second half-century it apparently decreased slightly, but after 1800 it rose again. For the last twenty-five years the age at admission to the Academical Department has been gradually increasing, until it is at present a little over 18½ years; the age at graduation is now, accordingly, a little over 22½ years. The youngest graduate, so far as known, is Charles Chauncey, who was graduated in 1792, at the age of 15 years and 26 days, and afterwards became a leading lawyer of Philadelphia.

Only two graduates have lived beyond a century: —the Rev. Nathan Birdseye, of Stratford, Conn., of the Class of 1736, born Aug. 19, 1714, died Jan. 28, 1818; and the Rev. Daniel Waldo, of Syracuse, N. Y., of the Class of 1788, born Sept. 10, 1762, died July 30, 1864.

The oldest surviving graduate at present is the Rev. David L. Hunn, of Buffalo, N. Y., of the Class of 1813, born Nov. 5, 1789.

The deaths of about 1800 graduates of the Academical Department have been reported since the Obituary Records began to be printed in 1859; and the average age of these at death has been 59.4 years.

The number of volumes (exclusive of unbound pamphlets) in the UNIVERSITY LIBRARY at various dates has been as follows:—1743, 2,600; 1766, 4,000;

1791, 2,700; 1808, 4,700; 1823, 6,620; 1835, 10,000; 1850, 21,000; 1860, 38,000; 1870, 55,000; 1880 (after the absorption of the Linonian and Brothers' Libraries), 120,000; 1887, 160,000.

The following is a list of the BUILDINGS at present occupied by the University, with the dates of their completion:—South Middle College, 1752; Athenaeum, 1763; Old Chemical Laboratory, 1782; South College, 1793; Lyceum, 1803; North Middle College, 1803; Sheffield Hall, first used as a Medical School in 1814; Reading Room (Old Cabinet), 1819; North College, 1821; Old Chapel, 1824; Treasury, 1832; Library, 1843; Alumni Hall, 1853; Gymnasium, 1859; Medical College, 1860; Art School, 1866; Farnam College, 1870; East Divinity Hall, 1870; Durfee College, 1871; Marquand Chapel, 1871; Law School, 1872; North Sheffield Hall, 1873; West Divinity Hall, 1874; Battell Chapel, 1876; Peabody Museum, 1876; Bacon Memorial Library, 1881; Observatory, 1882; Sloane Memorial Laboratory, 1883; Lawrance College, 1886; Dwight Hall, 1886; Kent Physical Laboratory, begun 1887.

Bibliography

A list follows of the more important published sources of information respecting the history of the University. Prices are added where the volumes are still in print.

The Annals or History of Yale-College, in New-Haven, . . . from the first Founding thereof, in the Year 1700, to the Year 1766 . . . By Thomas Clap, A.M., President of the said College. New Haven, 1766. 8°. pp. iv, 124.

A Sketch of the History of Yale College, in Connecticut. By Professor James L. Kingsley. In volume 8 of the American Quarterly Register, Boston, 1835-36, pp. 13-40, 201-18. 8°.

Annals of Yale College, from its Foundation, to the year 1831. By Ebenezer Baldwin. To which is added, an Appendix, bringing it down to 1838. 2d Edition. New Haven, 1838. 8°. pp. viii, 343.

An Historical Discourse pronounced before the Graduates of Yale College, August 14, 1850; One Hundred and Fifty Years after the Founding of that Institution . . . By Theodore D. Woolsey, President of Yale College. New Haven, 1850. 8°. pp. 128.

Yale College : a Sketch of its History, with Notices of its several Departments, Instructors, and Benefactors, together with some account of Student Life and Amusements, by various authors. Edited by William L. Kingsley. Illustrated with Views and Portraits. New York (Henry Holt & Co.), 1879. 2 vols. 4°. pp. xxvii, 504, + 76 pl.; and xvi, 533, + 88 pl. $20.

Appendix

Biographical Sketches of the Graduates of Yale College, with Annals of the College History: October, 1701—May, 1745. By Franklin Bowditch Dexter. New York (Henry Holt & Co.), 1885. 8°. pp. viii, 788. $5.
[A second volume, extending from 1745 to 1765, is in preparation.]

A Discourse, commemorative of the History of the Church of Christ in Yale College, during the First Century of its Existence. Preached in the College Chapel, Nov. 22, 1857. With Notes and an Appendix. By George P. Fisher, Livingston Professor of Divinity. New Haven, 1858. 8°. pp. 99.

A Statistical Account of the City of New Haven. By Timothy Dwight, President of Yale College.
New Haven, 1811. 8°. pp. 84.

The Semi-Centennial Anniversary of the Divinity School of Yale College, May 15 and 16, 1872. New Haven, 1872. 8°, pp. 119.

Historical Discourse by Theodore D. Woolsey, and Oration . . . by Hon. Edwards Pierrepont, LL.D., pronounced before the Alumni of the Law Department of Yale College, at the 50th Anniversary of the Foundation of the Department, . . . June 24, 1874. New Haven, 1874. 8°. pp. 47.

The Life of Ezra Stiles, D.D., LL.D., . . . President of Yale College. By Abiel Holmes. . . . Boston, 1798. 8°. pp. 404 + 1 pl.

Sketches of Yale College, with numerous anecdotes . . . By a Member of that Institution [E. P. Belden]. N. Y., 1843. 12°. pp. 192 + 4 pl.

Four Years at Yale. By a Graduate of '69 [L. H. Bagg]. New Haven, 1871. 12°. pp. xiv, 713.

Yale and "The City of Elms." By W. E. Decrow. Illustrated with Heliotypes . . . Boston, 1882. 12°. pp. xii, 131 + 15 pl. $1.50.

Since 1860 there has been published annually in Commencement week a pamphlet of the following series :—

Obituary Record of Graduates of Yale College deceased during the Academical Year ending in July, 1860—June, 1886.

Also, since 1868 another official pamphlet has appeared at the same anniversary, making a series entitled :—

Yale College in 1868-86. Some Statements respecting the late Progress and Present Condition of the various Departments of the University.

Many of the College Classes which have been graduated in recent years have printed for private circulation, at irregular intervals, Reports of their own history, in the form of biographical sketches. These pamphlets have been issued by the Class Secretaries, and a complete set is not easily found, except in the Library of the University. Such Reports have been printed for the Classes of 1797, 1802, 1810, 1813, 1816, 1817, 1819, 1821, 1822, 1824, 1826, 1830, 1832–76, 1878, 1879, 1881–83.

INDEX

Academical Department, name of	51	Catalogues, Annual, issues of	98
Addington, Isaac, draft of charter by	9	Triennial, issues of	98
		order of names in	39
Age at admission	100	Chapel, first	35
Allen, Oscar D., Professor	79	second	59
Alumni, age of	100	third (Battell)	85
catalogues of	98	Charter of 1701	9
funds raised by	60, 70, 81	1723	23
number of	98, 99	1745	28
in the Corporation	80	Chauncey, Nathaniel	13
Alumni Hall	69	Chittenden, Russell H., Professor	88
Andrew, Samuel, Rector	14	Chittenden, Simeon B., gifts of	67, 95
Art School, founding of	69	Church in College formed	35
progress of	89	Clap, Thomas, Rector, Administration of	27-37
Arts, Degrees in	13, 82	
Astronomical Observatory	86	Clark, John E., Professor	88
Athenaeum	35	Clark, Sheldon, gift of	65
Bacon, Francis, Professor	74, 93	Clarke, Wm. B., Professor	67
Bacon, Leonard, Rev. Dr.	72, 90	Coe, Edward B., Professor	67, 84
Baldwin, Simeon E., Professor	91	Commencement, the first	13
Barbour, Wm. M., Professor	84, 90	first in New Haven	17
Barker, Geo. F., Professor	74, 93	Commons, College	17, 44, 58
Battell Chapel	85	Connecticut, grants from	10, 11, 15, 22, 28, 34, 38, 45, 53, 60, 77
Beckwith, Frank E., Professor	93	
Beers, Henry A., Professor	83	legislative Acts of	9, 23, 28, 80, 94
Beers, Timothy, P., Professor	62, 74	need of College for	7
Berkeley, George, gifts of	25	representation of, in the Corporation	45, 80
Bissell, Clark, Professor	74	
Branford, Founders meet at	8	Corporation, constitution of the	10, 23, 29, 45, 80
Brastow, Lewis O., Professor	90	
Brewer, Wm. H., Professor	77	Cutler, Timothy, Rector	21, 22
Bristed, Charles A., gift of	68	Daggett, David, Professor	63, 74
Bronson, Henry, Professor	62, 74	Daggett, Naphtali, Professor	35
Brothers Society,	39, 87	President	38-40
Brush, Geo. J., Professor	76, 88	death of	42
Buckingham, Wm. A., gift of	72	Daggett, Oliver E., Professor	67
Buildings of the University	101	Dana, Edward S., Professor	83
Cabinet Building	58, 86	Dana, James D., Professor	66
Campbell, James, Professor	93	Davenport, John, Trustee	17
Carmalt, Wm. H., Professor	93	Davis, Henry, Rev. Dr.	55
Carter, Franklin, Professor	83, 84	Day, Geo. E., Professor	72

Index

Day, Jeremiah, Professor..........49, 50
  President......................55-64
  length of service of............ 97
DeForest, John, gift of............ 93
Degrees in Arts....................13, 82
  Divinity.......................... 73
  Engineering....................78, 88
  Law........................63, 92, 95
  Medicine......................... 51
  Philosophy.....................76, 78
Dexter, Franklin B., Professor.....71, 83
Divinity, Professorship of......... 35
Divinity school, buildings of ..62, 73, 90, 91
  degrees in....................... 73
  origin of......................52, 61
  progress of....................71, 90
DuBois, A. Jay, Professor.......... 89
Dummer, Jeremiah, gifts through.14, 18
Durfee, Bradford M. C., gifts of..66, 69
Dutton, Henry, Professor.......... 74
Dutton, Matthew R., Professor... 57
Dwight, Timothy, the elder, President.......................47-54
  the younger, Professor........ 71
  President........................ 94
Dwight Hall......................... 86
Eaton, D. Cady, Professor......70, 89
Eaton, Daniel C., Professor....... 78
Elective studies.................... 82
Ellsworth, Henry L., gift of....... 85
English, James E., gift of......... 91
Episcopacy, defection to........... 22
Faculty, powers of..............47, 56
Fagging abolished.................. 48
Farnam, Henry W., Professor.... 89
Farnam College..................... 69
Fellows, Alumni representation in 80
  qualifications of....10, 23, 29, 45, 80
  State representation in........45, 80
  term of office of................. 97
Fine Arts, School of. See ART SCHOOL.
Fisher, Alexander M., Professor..56, 57
Fisher, Geo. P., Professor......66, 72
Fitch, Eleazar T., Professor.56, 61, 66, 71
Foster, LaFayette S., gift of...... 92
Gibbs, Josiah W., Professor.....62, 71
Gibbs, J. Willard, Professor...... 83

Gilman, Daniel C., Professor..71, 77, 88
Gooch, Frank A., Professor...... 95
Goodrich, Chauncey A., Professor 56, 57, 62, 71
Goodrich, Elizur, Professor....... 50
Graduate Department, organization of............................63, 75
  progress of....................81, 93
Graduates. See ALUMNI.
Gymnasium......................... 70
Hadley, Arthur T., Professor..... 93
Hadley, Henry H., Professor..... 72
Hadley, James, Professor.......66, 84
Harper, Wm. R., Professor....... 93
Harris, Samuel, Professor......... 72
Hartford, plan of removal to....16, 17
Harvard College................. 7, 13
Hastings, Charles S., Professor... 88
Heminway, Jacob................. 13
Herrick, Edward C...........62, 70, 71
Higgin, Mrs. Susan K., gift of.... 79
Hillhouse, James, treasurer......45, 60
Hooker, Charles, Professor......62, 74
Hooker, Worthington, Professor . 74
Hoppin, James M., Professor..72, 89, 90
Hubbard, Stephen G., Professor..74, 93
Hubbard, Thomas, Professor..... 62
Ives, Charles L., Professor......74, 93
Ives, Eli, Professor.............51, 73
Jewett, Pliny A., Professor....... 74
Johnson, Samuel, Rev. Dr........ 25
Johnson, Samuel W., Professor... 76
Kent, Albert E., gift of........... 95
Killingworth, the School at....... 14
Kingsley, Henry C., treasurer....70, 94
Kingsley, James L., Professor...49, 50, 56, 66, 97
Knapp, Wm. I., Professor........ 84
Knight, Jonathan, Professor...51, 74, 97
Ladd, Geo. T., Professor......... 83
Langdon, Solomon, gift of........ 60
Larned, Wm. A., Professor......57, 67
Larned, Mrs. Wm. A., gift of..... 87
Lathrop, Daniel, gift of........... 44
Law School, degrees in........63, 92, 95
  gifts to.....................91, 92, 95
  origin of......................52, 62
  progress of................74, 91, 95
Lawrance College.................. 85

Index 107

Lewis, Addin, gift of 71
Library, beginning of 8
   catalogue of 37
   early gifts to 14, 18, 25
   funds of 44, 53, 59, 87
   location of 17, 35, 52, 59, 95
   losses of 20, 44
   volumes in 100
Lindsley, Charles A., Professor .. 74
Linonian Society 40, 87
Linsly, Noah, gift of 59
Livingston, Philip, gift of 34
Lockwood, James, chosen President 38
Lockwood, Samuel, gifts of 44
Loomis, Elias, Professor 67
Lounsbury, Thomas R., Professor 79
Lyceum 52
Lyman, Chester S., Professor 77
Marquand, Frederick, gifts of 90
Marsh, Ebenezer G., instructor... 50
Marsh, Othniel C., Professor 80
Mather, Cotton, letter of 18
Medical School, buildings of ... 51, 74
   origin of 51
   progress of 62, 73, 92
Meigs, Josiah, Professor 46, 50
Mixter, Wm. G., Professor 88
Monroe, Elbert B., gift of 86
Morgan, Henry T., gift of 84
Names, family, of alumni 98
New Haven, call for College in... 8
   removal to 16
Newton, Hubert A., Professor ... 67
Niemeyer, John H., Professor 89
North College 59
North Middle College 52
Northrop, Cyrus, Professor 67, 84
Norton, John P., Professor 75, 76
Norton, John T., gift of 59
Norton, Wm. A., Professor 76
Obituary Record 100, 104
Observatory 86
Olmsted, Denison, Professor .. 57, 67
Osborne, Thomas B., Professor... 74
Otis, Asa, gift of 91
Packard, Lewis R., Professor... 66, 84
Peabody Museum, erection of.... 86
   gift of 80

Peck, Tracy, Professor 83
Perkins, Alfred E., gift of 59
Phelps, Edward J., Professor..... 83
Phelps, John Jay, gift of 87
Phillips, Andrew W., Professor .. 83
Philosophy and the Arts, Department of, degrees in 76, 78, 82, 88
   organization of 75, 81
Pierpont, James, Trustee 8, 10
Pierson, Abraham, Rector ...8, 9, 13, 14
Platt, Johnson T., Professor 91
Porter, John A., Professor 76
Porter, Noah, Professor 65, 72
   President 81-93
Porter, T. Dwight, gift of 84
President, powers of 33
   term of office of 97
President's House, first 21, 53
   second 53, 69, 75
Professors, length of life of 98
Professorship, first 35
Prudential Committee 25
Rector made a Trustee 23
Religious worship in College 34
Revolution, effects of the 41-44
Richards, Charles B., Professor... 89
Richards, Eugene L., Professor... 83
Robinson, Wm. C., Professor 91
Rockwell, Alfred P., Professor ... 78
Russell, John E., Professor 90
Russell, Thomas H., Professor ... 93
Sage, Henry W., gift of 73
Salisbury, Edward E., Professor 63, 75, 79
   gifts of 71, 79
Salter, Richard, gift of 43
Saltonstall, Gurdon, Governor.... 17
Sanford, Leonard J., Professor ... 74
Saybrook, the College at 13-15
   removal from 16, 19
Scientific School, named 76
   progress of 77, 88
Sewall, Samuel, Judge 9
Seymour, Thomas D., Professor.. 84
Sheffield, Joseph E., gifts of 77, 89
Sheffield Hall 77, 78
Sheffield Hall, North 79
Sheffield Scientific School, named. 77
   progress of 78, 88

108   Index

Silliman, Benj., Professor..49, 50, 51, 66, 73, 97
Silliman, Benj., Jr., Professor..74, 75, 93
Sloane Laboratory.................. 85
Smith, David P., Professor........ 93
Smith, Herbert E., Professor..... 93
Smith, Nathan, Professor..........51, 62
Smith, Sidney I., Professor....... 88
South College...................... 46
South Middle College.............. 34
Stanley, Anthony D., Professor ..57, 67
Staples, Seth P., Law School of...52, 63
Stiles, Ezra, President............ 41
   instruction by 42, 43
   death of 46
Storrs, Wm. L., Professor.........63, 74
Street, Augustus R., gifts of...67, 69, 72
Strong, Nehemiah, Professor.....39, 42
Students, numbers of............43, 60, 98
Sumner, Wm. G., Professor....... 83
Taylor, Nathaniel W., Professor.61, 62, 71
Tests imposed on officers..........22, 46
Thacher, James K., Professor..... 93
Thacher, Thomas A., Professor ..56, 83
Theological Department. See Divinity School.
Townsend, Isaac H., Professor...63, 74
Townsend, Wm. K., Professor ... 92
Treasury Building..............59, 60, 70
Triennial Catalogue. See Catalogue.
Trinity College....................54, 61

Trowbridge, Henry, gift of....... 73
Trowbridge, Wm. P., Professor..79, 89
Trumbull Gallery 59, 60, 70
Trustees. See Fellows.
Tuition, rates of..................... 68
Tully, Wm., Professor 62
University funds 81
   name legalized................... 94
   principle adopted 53
Van Name, Addison, librarian....71, 72
Verrill, Addison E., Professor.... 77
Visitation by the Legislature 36
Wales, Samuel, Professor 43
Walker, Francis A., Professor.... 88
Warner, Wyllys, treasurer 60, 70
Wayland, Francis, Professor..... 91
Weir, John F., Professor.......... 70
Wethersfield, students at 16, 17
Wheeler, Arthur M., Professor... 66
White, Moses C., Professor 74
Whitney, Wm. D., Professor..... 76
Wilcox, Lucian S., Professor 93
Williams, Elisha, Rector 16, 24-27
Winchester, Oliver F., gift of..... 87
Winkley, Henry, gift of 91
Woolsey, Theodore D., Professor 56; 58
   President......................65-80
Woolsey, Theodore S., Professor. 92
Woolsey Fund 81
Wright, Arthur W., Professor.... 83
Wright, Henry P., Professor..... 83
Yale, Elihu, gifts of 15, 18, 21
   sketch of......................... 1

www.ingramcontent.com/pod-product-compliance
Lightning Source LLC
Chambersburg PA
CBHW031409160426
43196CB00007B/953